A THIRTY-ONE DAY DEVOTIONAL

ENDURING GRACE

Testimonies of the Extraordinary Power of
the Gospel in the Lives of Ordinary Christians

J. AARON WHITE

REDEEMER
BIBLE CHURCH

This book is dedicated to Mrs. Robin Johnson. Without her gracious and tireless efforts, this project would not have been possible. Thank you, Robin, for serving Redeemer Bible Church and being a living example of God's enduring grace.

CONTENTS

FOREWORD

Every story of a redeemed life is a bold declaration of the goodness and grace of God. Stories of redemption have played an important role at Redeemer Bible Church—especially over the past five years. Each membership class begins with every person sharing their testimony of faith in Christ. Before someone enters the waters of baptism, they tell the gathered congregation how Christ has rescued them. When new members are added to the Redeemer faith family, time is carved out in the main worship service, and together God's people celebrate the faithfulness of the Lord who has sovereignly called sinners of all kinds to find new life in Christ.

As a church, we are indebted to our brother, Aaron, for taking the time to help the members of Redeemer tell their stories. As I've read through each testimony, I've been profoundly encouraged. I've worshipped as I've read. I've stopped mid-story with tears in my eyes and thanked the Lord for his staggering kindness. These stories have fueled my hope in Christ, and they have motivated me to tell others of his death and resurrection.

My prayer is that this special book will be used by every Redeemer member and every Redeemer family. These are the gloriously true stories of the people that surround you every Sunday. These are the stories of those that lift their voices with you in praise and worship each week.

Charles Spurgeon captures the heart behind this book when he writes, *"I received some years ago orders from my Master to stand at the foot of the cross until he came. He has not come yet, but I mean to stand there till he does. If I should disobey his orders and leave those simple truths which have been the means of the conversion of souls, I know not how I could expect his blessing.*

Here, then, I stand at the foot of the cross and tell out the old, old story, stale though it sound to itching ears, and worn threadbare as critics may deem it. It is of Christ I love to speak— of Christ who loved, and lived, and died, the substitute for sinners, the just for the unjust, that he might bring us to God."

Brothers and sisters, this is really a book about the person and work of Christ. This is a book designed to deepen your love for Jesus. So, now, open this small book and hear the old, old story—rehearsed on every page.

Sustained by his enduring grace,

Jason Wredberg

Redeemer Bible Church
Minnetonka, MN
March, 2022

INTRODUCTION

The impulse that brought this book into existence was one of personal and pastoral concern. The Lord has mercifully sustained my faith amid seasons of anxiety and depression, and he saw fit to use the testimonies of other believers as means to that end. In one particularly dark period, I found strength by supplementing my study of Scripture with the reading of Arnold Dallimore's masterful biography of Charles Spurgeon.[1] Despite being the Prince of Preachers, it was Spurgeon's personal struggles that proved to be balm to my fractured soul. In his battles against depression, anxiety, fear, doubt, physical pain, and loneliness, Charles' hope rested in the grace of God in Christ Jesus. Although vicarious, my observation of Spurgeon's life and the power of the gospel to sustain him provided me with strength to press on in my own race of faith—and I remain eternally grateful. Gaining strength from observing God's grace in the lives of others is precisely what the author of the Book of Hebrews intended when he wrote: "Therefore, since we are surrounded by so great a cloud of witnesses... let us run with endurance the race that is set before us" (Heb. 12:1).[2] All the names mentioned in chapter 11 are included in this "cloud of witnesses." These are people who finished the race of faith and made it home to glory, sinners who were sustained by God's unfailing, enduring grace. Abraham, Moses, David, Spurgeon, and countless other saints whose names will never be known until eternity continue to serve us today. Their lives bear witness to the unfailing love of

---

1 Arnold A. Dallimore, *Spurgeon: A Biography* (Carlisle, PA: The Banner of Truth Trust, 2014).

2 Unless otherwise noted, all Scripture references are from The English Standard Version (Wheaton, IL: Crossway, 2016).

God and his sovereign prerogative to sustain and empower his children amid hardship and calamity.

The same grace that sustained Charles Spurgeon has come with equal power in the lives of other, lesser-known saints. One of my pastoral concerns that gave rise to *Enduring Grace* was the prospect of losing the testimonies of older believers. Their accounts of God's enduring grace through the trials of life are gold mines of spiritual encouragement for younger readers. Sadly, many of their stories will never be known this side of eternity. The strength and encouragement that could have come to the next generation of Christians have been lost to the piercing silence of the grave. Too often have I laid a dear elderly saint to rest knowing that their testimony will never reach the ears of younger Christians. The power of the gospel that sustained them through marriage, parenting, loss, fear, and sickness would doubtless prove medicinal to anyone who would learn of it.

As the title and subtitle imply, this book is intended to be used as a daily devotional. The individuals cited are real, and their stories were captured in firsthand interviews. Though the ultimate aim of *Enduring Grace* is to glorify God for the sustaining power of his gospel, it also seeks to honor the lives and stories of the beloved saints whose names appear in the chapter headings. The intended audience of this book Christians who seek to persevere in faith and run their race with Christ-centered intensity. Each chapter contains the testimony of an older Christian, their advice to younger readers, and a favorite passage of Scripture. Whether the reader is a new Christian bursting with zeal, or a seasoned soldier wounded in battle, *Enduring Grace* seeks to provide Christ-exalting strength and encouragement.

In addition to the exhortation of Hebrews 12, this book is also informed by Paul's words to the Philippian believers:

Not that I have already obtained this or am already perfect, but I press on to make it my own, because Christ Jesus has made me his own. Brothers, I do not consider that I have made it my own. But one thing I do: forgetting what lies behind and straining forward to what lies ahead, I press on toward the goal for the prize of the upward call of God in Christ Jesus. Let those of us who are mature think this way, and if in anything you think otherwise, God will reveal that also to you. Only let us hold true to what we have attained. *Brothers, join in imitating me, and keep your eyes on those who walk according to the example you have in us* (Phil. 3:12-17, emphasis added).

This is precisely the hope of this book. May the Lord grant you his enduring grace as you learn of the extraordinary power of the gospel in the lives of ordinary Christians.

By Grace Alone,

J. Aaron White

DEVOTIONALS

DAY 1

DOUG (B.1935)

LOVE, LOSS, AND LIFE ETERNAL

It was that sublime moment when a once-cherished existence gives way to the cascading rush of a more impending reality. Ann's simple confession echoed in Doug's mind like a hammer being dropped in an empty gymnasium. She came home after another meeting with the ladies at what was supposed to be a yawn-inducing Bible study and said, "I don't think I have ever really placed my trust in Jesus Christ." Doug was stymied. Though he was raised in a Lutheran church and confirmed at a young age, Doug married Ann and they began attending a Presbyterian church. Unlike the other laity who smugly embraced a passive consumerism, Doug and Ann served the church by teaching Sunday school. They never questioned their status before God because they both knew that teaching a Bible class was surely enough to garner a smile from the Almighty. So, why would Ann come home and make such a startling proclamation?

She was the love of his life, his best friend. Doug met Ann while attending the University of Minnesota. They went to campus events together and their relationship blossomed. They married and soon began raising children. Ann was resting in the hospital after delivering their third son, and the lady sharing Ann's room was listening to a cassette of a man preaching from the Bible. She invited Ann to listen in, and soon after she joined the woman's

Bible study group. Despite serving in a local church, Ann finally heard the gospel of Jesus Christ clearly at the women's study group. Over time, Doug himself began listening to the preaching tapes and attending a Bible study group. Like Ann, he came to realize that he was a sinner in desperate need of a Savior. Teaching an eternity of Sunday school classes would never pay off Doug's sin debt; he needed Jesus to be his Lord and Savior. With newfound zeal, Ann and Doug committed themselves to a small group Bible study that would later become Redeemer Bible Church in Minnetonka, Minnesota. Of his salvation, Doug said that the Spirit of God "turned [his] life upside down." He was amazed that after thirty years of attending church, his eyes were opened to the glory of Jesus Christ through the power of the gospel.

Ann and Doug attended church regularly, no longer serving to win favor with God but serving out of an overflow of joy in God's grace. The apostle Paul highlights the reality of this kind of grace-fueled service. After laboring for eleven chapters of dense theology, he calls upon his readers to respond: "I appeal to you therefore, brothers, *by the mercies of God*, to present your bodies as a living sacrifice, holy and acceptable to God, which is your spiritual worship" (Rom. 12:1, emphasis added). This is precisely how Doug and Ann came to view their involvement in church—a joyful response to God's sovereign grace. The vivacity of his marriage compounded his grief when he learned that his beloved Ann developed an aggressive lung cancer. Her treatments made her ill, and Doug prayed earnestly for her healing and recovery. Yet the winds of providence blew Doug's vessel into menacing waters. Ann succumbed to the cancer. Nevertheless, God sustained Doug and enabled him to say: "I witnessed God's grace when [he] gave me the faith to see that my request had been answered. Ann was healed in heaven." Seeing his beloved Ann slip away, Doug rested in the blood-bought reality that "though our outer self is wasting away, our inner self is being renewed day by day. For this light momentary affliction is preparing for us an eternal weight of glory beyond all comparison" (2 Cor. 4:16b-17).

Ann's death was not the only occasion on which Doug relied on God's enduring grace to sustain him. Though it provided an income, owning a family business often pressed Doug into the dust of despair. On one occasion, Doug recalled when the secretary reminded him that the employees' health insurance payments had to be made by week's end. In truth, there was no money available. The gospel of grace had turned the once self-reliant man into a God-dependent man. Doug prayed, and the Lord graciously provided for his needs. Some of his customers decided to pay their bills early, supplying his business with the much-needed funds in time to pay his employees. Suffice to say, God always provided for Doug's needs and trained him in the school of prayer along the way. As of the writing of this book, Doug's three sons still own and operate the family business, an enterprise sustained by prayer and God's provision.

ADVICE TO YOUNGER READERS: Remember that the things of this world are temporary; they pass away quickly. The world is full of temptations, so guard your heart. Don't waste your life on things that will never satisfy—the things of God give eternal joy!

FAVORITE PASSAGE: "For I am sure that neither death nor life, nor angels nor rulers, nor things present nor things to come, nor powers, nor height nor depth, nor anything else in all creation, will be able to separate us from the love of God in Christ Jesus our Lord" (Rom. 8:38-39).

DAY 2

EVA (B.1934)

A HERITAGE OF GRACE

A young farmer kneels next to his weathered tractor in a solemn moment of prayer. Though this scene is reminiscent of a Norman Rockwell painting, it is one that took place when a pastor came to visit a young man while he was working in the fields of a farm. Eva's dad was the proverbial salt of the earth. The gospel of Jesus Christ came into his life with saving power, and he joyfully recounted his testimony the remainder of his days. The young farmer went on to raise eight children, and Eva counts one of her most cherished memories as the sound of her father singing hymns while out in the fields. As familiar lines from *Amazing Grace* and *It Is Well* echoed through the cornstalks, they made their way to Eva's ears—and her tender heart. The young farmer grew to be the embodiment of the psalmist's words: "So even to old age and gray hairs, O God, do not forsake me, until I proclaim your might to another generation, your power to all those to come" (Ps. 71:18).

While in junior high, Eva attended a Vacation Bible School and heard the gospel. In God's sovereign timing, he opened her eyes to see the depth of her sin, her need of a Savior, and the sufficiency of God's provided Lamb, the Lord Jesus Christ. Her father's faithful example of God-centered joy propelled her toward her own experience of grace, and she was soon baptized. After high school, Eva met Jerry. They both worked at a local hardware store, and Jerry coached Eva's softball team. The two were married and started a family, something that Jerry greatly cherished. He would often communicate how important family was and worked to ensure that they did things together as a group. If dinner at a restaurant was the plan, Jerry made sure that the entire family was able to go. It was his love of family that informed his decision to purchase a motor home. Jerry and Eva's children were allowed to choose the campsite, and they always made sure to find one with a pool. The motor home provided Eva's growing family with many miles of scenery and even more precious memories.

In January of 1992, Eva's beloved Jerry fell ill. His symptoms pointed to a nagging flu, but test results soon revealed that Jerry had advanced cancer that was attacking his liver. After years of joyful marriage, Eva knew that her Jerry would soon be taken away. For the Christian, the prospect of death is always a paradoxical affair, one marked by being "sorrowful, yet always rejoicing" (2 Cor. 6:10). Such was Eva's experience. The doctors gave Jerry only a few weeks to live, but God's mercy abounded and granted the two lovers another nine months together. Eva saw the extension of Jerry's life as God's grace to her, and she was exceedingly thankful. Jerry went home to be with the Lord he loved and served, but Eva pressed on in faith and trusted God to sustain and protect her in Jerry's absence. The Good Shepherd looked after his beloved lamb, providing the means for Eva to move back into the home where she and Jerry had raised their children. This was a place pregnant with fond memories, and Eva was overjoyed to nestle back into familiar surroundings. The walls of Eva's home tell the story of the gospel's power in the lives of two sinners who found unshakable joy in their mutual Savior. Photos of Eva, Jerry, their children, and their grandchildren are silent monuments to the enduring grace of God.

Losing a beloved spouse is a reality with which many saints are confronted this side of heaven. Yet the sting of death, for the Christian, is blunted by the hope of eternal life with Christ. Eva remains in good health and is an active member of a local Bible church where she attends and serves regularly. The grace of God continues to sustain her, and she opens her home and heart to others. The grace-fueled example of Eva's perseverance is captured by the apostle Paul: "For by grace you have been saved through faith. And this is not your own doing; it is the gift of God, not a result of works, so that no one may boast. For we are his workmanship, created in Christ Jesus for good works, which God prepared beforehand, that we should walk in them" (Eph. 2:8-10). The grace that came to her father in the middle of a field also came to Eva. The power of the gospel that moved a young farmer to spend his days singing the praises of his Lord also moved Eva to press on in faith amid blessings and hardship. Eva's heritage of grace is available to all who will likewise repent of their sins and trust in the Lord Jesus Christ.

ADVICE TO YOUNGER READERS: Take time to do family devotions and eat your meals together without cell phones, electronics, or other distractions. Also, be honest with your children about your own sins and let them know about your need of (and love for) the Savior. When you sin against them or your spouse, seek forgiveness and restoration humbly and quickly.

FAVORITE PASSAGE: "Trust in the Lord with all your heart, and do not lean on your own understanding" (Prov. 3:5).

DAY 3

JEAN (B.1956)

TRUSTING CHRIST AMID THE TEARS

It's scary how easily we can be deluded. Like Nero fiddling a dirge while Rome burned to the ground, we can fool ourselves into thinking that we are right with God when we are, in fact, under his righteous wrath. Such was the case with young Jean. Despite growing up in a Christian home and possessing a solid foundation of biblical knowledge, she remained in love with her sin and her sense of autonomy. In her own insightful words, Jean said, "I knew it was all true and never questioned what I was taught from an early age. I just figured that as long as I believed, I was good to go...But that still didn't keep me from wanting to do things my own way and living a sinful lifestyle." The prophet Isaiah summarized the condition of Jean and a sad host of others: "...this people draw near with their mouth and honor me with their lips, while their hearts are far from me, and their fear of me is a commandment taught by men" (Isa. 29:13). In her late twenties, however, the grace of God overcame her rebellion and Jean was truly saved. While attending a local church and hearing the gospel, Jean said that "Jesus turned the light on, and my life changed forever...My eyes were opened to how sinful I really was, and how badly I needed his healing power in my heart."

Attending a church that valued expositional preaching was critical for Jean. Sitting under the regular unfolding and application of God's Word put steel in her spiritual backbone. This would prove to be critical as Jean's first husband left her, and it was her church family that became her source of support and a crucial means of grace in her life as a divorcee. Years later, another wave of pain crashed over Jean's life when she lost a fiancé to cancer. Like many of God's children, Jean found solace in the psalms amid her tears. A passage of particular comfort in her mourning was Psalm 91: "He who dwells in the shelter of the Most High will abide in the shadow of the Almighty. I will say to the Lord, 'My refuge and my fortress, my God, in whom I trust'" (Ps. 91:1-2). Trusting God in seasons of blessing is relatively easy. It is in the seasons of confusion, despair, and fear that faith is forged in the Master's fire. Perhaps one of the most insidious enemies of a Christian's faith is fear. Jean battled fear by swimming in the psalms and preaching them to her own trembling heart. Think of what a storehouse of faith-strengthening comfort is found there:

"I love you, O Lord, my strength. The Lord is my rock and my fortress and my deliverer, my God, my rock, in whom I take refuge, my shield, and the horn of my salvation, my stronghold" (Ps. 18:1-2).

"Blessed be the Lord! For he has heard the voice of my pleas for mercy. The Lord is my strength and my shield; in him my heart trusts, and I am helped; my heart exults, and with my song I give thanks to him" (Ps. 28:6-7).

"I waited patiently for the Lord; he inclined to me and heard my cry. He drew me up from the pit of destruction, out of the miry bog, and set my feet upon a rock, making my steps secure. He put a new song in my mouth, a song of praise to our God. Many will see and fear, and put their trust in the Lord" (Ps. 40:1-3).

Jean knew that in Christ all these promises were hers. She rested in her Savior and waited for his hand to lead her. She finally remarried and continues to trust in her Savior for sustaining grace, though much of her pain has now passed. God's grace in the past assures her of his enduring grace for her future. The tears of days gone by have trained Jean to live in a constant attitude of humble dependence upon Christ, communing with him in prayer continuously. She has come to know and treasure what the author of Hebrews declared: "For we do not have a high priest who is unable to sympathize with our weaknesses, but one who in every respect has been tempted as we are, yet without sin. Let us then with confidence draw near to the throne of grace, that we may receive mercy and find grace to help in time of need" (Heb. 4:15-16).

ADVICE TO YOUNGER READERS: Talk to the Lord no matter what is going on in your life. Whether you are anxious, fearful, worried, angry, or joyful, take everything to him in prayer. Most importantly, thank him for everything. Even if things seem unclear, he is sovereign and in control.

FAVORITE PASSAGE: "Satisfy us in the morning with your steadfast love, that we may rejoice and be glad all our days" (Ps. 90:14).

DAY 4

JIM (B.1932)

SATURATED WITH SCRIPTURE

The strength of metal is tested under pressure. Its integrity is affirmed when it remains intact and uncompromised in the face of extreme weight and heat. The Son of God bore the infinite weight of God's wrath while hanging on the cross. As the hand of divine justice pressed the substitutionary Lamb, the very thing that the sinless Son of God lived on poured forth. Rather than curses or anger, Scripture instinctively bellowed from the Messiah: "My God, my God, why have you forsaken me?" (Ps. 22:1). As the God-Man, Jesus lived in daily communion with his Father. One of the means by which he did this was feasting upon Scripture: "It is written, 'Man shall not live by bread alone, but by every word that comes from the mouth of God'" (Matt. 4:4). It is no surprise that when the Son of God was crushed under God's righteous judgment for the sins of his people, the aroma of Scripture filled the air. Like the Master, every Christian is called to feast upon and relish God's Word: "Blessed is the man who walks not in the counsel of the wicked, nor stands in the way of sinners, nor sits in the seat of scoffers; but his delight is in the law of the Lord, and on his law he meditates day and night" (Ps. 1:1-2). It is the blessed man, the one who has tasted the grace of God, whose renewed heart and mind find joy in God's unfailing Word.

Jim is such a man. Like his Lord, Jim bleeds Bible. Raised in a Christian home, he attended Sunday school throughout his childhood. The seeds of the gospel that were sown into his life came to flower in his teens. It was then that Jim was awakened to the reality of his sin and the predicament in which he found himself with a holy God. By God's grace, he found forgiveness by faith alone in Christ alone. During his college years, Jim attended classes on Christian worldview and Bible surveys and found his hunger to study Scripture increasing rapidly. He married the love of his life, Betty, and the two soon began hosting a home Bible study that would later become a thriving local church in the suburbs of Minneapolis. Throughout Jim's life, the Word of God has been his delight and constant pursuit. Early on in Jim's home study, a Christian professor was invited to teach them for a week. Using a reel-to-reel machine, Jim and the others recorded the lectures and listened to them repeatedly. Such was their hunger for the milk and meat of God's Word.

Jim studied alongside the growing number of hungry believers who met multiple times during the week to examine Scripture together. Through the years, he served as an elder, deacon, and treasurer for the steadily expanding church. The role of media in Jim's spiritual growth cannot be understated. Before the advent of the Internet, podcasts, and live streaming, Jim's hunger for Scripture drove him to make use of every means of accessing solid Bible teaching available to him. Jim's love for Christ was fueled by a steady diet of biblical intake. Like the psalmist, Jim could say: "Teach me, O Lord, the way of your statutes; and I will keep it to the end. Give me understanding, that I may keep your law and observe it with my whole heart. Lead me in the path of your commandments, for I delight in it" (Ps. 119:33-35). Jim's marriage to Betty has been sweetened by their joint pursuit of knowing God's Word. Despite aging bodies, they continue to relish God's Word and have come to taste the joy of seeing their children and grandchildren embrace the gospel also. Jim continues to shepherd his growing family, serving as an example of God's marvelous, sustaining grace. He and Betty help each other memorize Scripture on their daily walks. Like his Master, Jim bleeds Bible. He has immersed himself in the pursuit of being saturated with Scripture, an endeavor that has reaped rich rewards for Jim and the countless believers he has impacted.

ADVICE TO YOUNGER READERS: Not surprisingly, Jim's counsel is summed up in the following succinct exhortation—read your Bibles! There are countless activities in our lives that can be set aside but soaking in the Word of God is not one of them. In addition to personal study and memorization, regular attendance at a Bible-saturated, Christ-centered local church is vital as well as regularly confessing our sin and resting in Christ.

FAVORITE PASSAGE: "Bless the Lord, O my soul, and all that is within me, bless his holy name! Bless the Lord, O my soul, and forget not all his benefits, who forgives all your iniquity, who heals all your diseases, who redeems your life from the pit, who crowns you with steadfast love and mercy, who satisfies you with good so that your youth is renewed like the eagle's" (Ps. 103:1-5).

DAY 5

MARLENE (B.1938)

FREE AT LAST!

In the 1992 thriller *A Few Good Men*, actor Jack Nicholson shouted a line that has become part of modern parlance: "You can't handle the truth!" With an economy of words, this phrase summarizes Marlene's plight. Her parents owned a nursery that was open seven days a week, so they sent her to church with her grandma. Marlene learned various Bible stories and became convinced of God's existence early in her life. She recalls sitting in church, praying that God would show her how to get to heaven. While attending college, Marlene joined a group for Christian students but was perplexed by its teaching. The group focused on biblical topics, so Marlene's interest was piqued. However, when the specifics of the gospel were discussed, she began avoiding the conversation because it scared her. It was her aversion to the gospel that made her realize that she was not a Christian. To her dismay, she couldn't handle the truth. The apostle Paul describes Marlene's predicament this way: "For the mind that is set on the flesh is hostile to God, for it does not submit to God's law; indeed, it cannot. Those who are in the flesh cannot please God" (Rom. 8:7-8).

After shopping with a close friend, Marlene returned home and found a gospel tract in her bag. The Lord used the medium of a simple pamphlet to begin opening Marlene's eyes and heart to the truth of the gospel. In her excitement, she scheduled a meeting with a pastor. This encounter, however, would prove to be a massive disappointment as the pastor glibly replied, "Marlene,

I think you're a good person." Dissatisfied and committed to knowing the truth, Marlene invited a Christian couple over one evening. It was during that visit that her search for biblical truth ended, the glory and supremacy of Christ became clear, and her fears were finally allayed. Shortly thereafter, the shy and often quiet Marlene married the outgoing and energetic Don. The two enjoyed hosting guests in their home and traveling abroad for Don's work. Aside from her love for Christ, her greatest earthly joy was her sweet husband. They complimented one another, and Don would gently lead and care for Marlene through the shifting seasons of life. It was the happiness of their marriage that has made widowhood a perennial trial for Marlene, but she sees God's enduring grace continually at work in her life. The Lord who began a good work in her in her younger years continues that work today (Phil. 1:6)—and he promises to complete it.

A particular trial that has driven Marlene to the throne room of mercy has been the physical ailment of her son, Mike. After developing flu-like symptoms and prolonged fatigue, Mike was eventually diagnosed with Lyme disease. Marlene interceded for her son, a young husband and soon-to-be-father. Her son's emotions were understandably volatile, and Marlene spent much time in prayer for her family. Walking with a sick loved one often brings fresh insight into Paul's words: "Likewise the Spirit helps us in our weakness. For we do not know what to pray for as we ought, but the Spirit himself intercedes for us with groanings too deep for words" (Rom. 8:26). Yet Marlene's prayers have routinely been answered as she sees God's grace in her life as well as Mike's.

A tumultuous journey to faith in Christ, a blissful marriage, an ailing adult child, and the grief of losing a spouse—all took place under the watchful and loving eye of a sovereign God. Marlene continues to marvel at the ways, big and small, the Good Shepherd provides and cares for her. She knows her Lord's words to be trustworthy: "Therefore do not be anxious, saying, 'What shall we eat?' or 'What shall we drink?' or 'What shall we wear?' For the Gentiles seek after all these things, and your heavenly Father knows that you need them all. But seek first the kingdom of God and his righteousness, and all these things will be added to you" (Matt. 6:31-33). Marlene continues to rejoice in her blood-bought freedom in Christ and the Spirit-empowered ability to handle the only truth that matters.

ADVICE TO YOUNGER READERS: Make sure to stay in God's Word; this is your daily food. Moreover, make the study of God's attributes a priority in your life as it will build your trust in him. As you come to know and love him more deeply, the spiritual disciplines will become a joy rather than a burden. Read and meditate upon Scripture, applying it to yourself personally and humbly.

FAVORITE PASSAGE: "For our sake he made him to be sin who knew no sin, so that in him we might become the righteousness of God" (2 Cor. 5:21).

DAY 6

PATTIE (B.1938)

OVERFLOWING JOY

Effervescent. This is the only word in the English language that accurately captures the bubbly, enthusiastic spirit that Pattie embodies. Yet, the smiling woman who loves to greet churchgoers as they enter the building was not always so... effervescent. Like many others, Pattie lived much of her life in a respectably moral fashion. She and her husband, Paul, grew up with a rudimentary knowledge of the Bible and the key tenets of Christianity. They married in 1960 and moved to Maryland for Paul's job, one of many moves that his career would demand from their growing family. The various shades of Pattie's life have been colored by pain. In addition to numerous moves and the strain of being uprooted, Pattie also endured several miscarriages and a breast cancer diagnosis in 2010 that resulted in a double mastectomy. Despite all these things, she is rightly described as, well, effervescent. What is the wellspring of Pattie's indomitable, overflowing joy? As with many acts of divine providence, it began in an unlikely place—a country club in Washington, D. C.

After moving to Bethesda, Maryland, a group of ladies in Pattie's neighborhood invited her to attend a Bible study. Pattie knew these ladies self-identified as *born-again Christians*, though she herself was unsure of what that meant. One of the early studies was held at Pattie's house, an event that served as a catalyst to propel her into deeper, more serious study of the Scriptures. It was this group of ladies who brought Pattie to the luncheon in

D. C., and it was at that luncheon that God called Pattie to himself. In her own words, Pattie describes that life-changing afternoon:

I had been striving a good part of my life to please God and know him, but he spoke to my heart and mind through the speaker that day and claimed me for his own! I had never heard the gospel presented before like this; I realized that I desperately needed forgiveness for my sins and that, through Christ, I could receive that forgiveness…I was bowled over, but I felt a bit self-conscious as the speaker asked those who would like to receive the gift of Christ…to mark our place cards and speak to her after the luncheon. I did both [and I] felt overwhelmed with gratitude and excitement; I couldn't wait to call Paul and tell him that God had saved me and promised to sanctify and prepare me to see him one day face to face in heaven!

Pattie's newfound joy would soon be tempered as she returned to the Episcopal church that she and Paul attended. She asked her pastor to visit their home so that she could share the exciting news of her salvation with him, a man who would surely share in her joy. However, the pastor fielded Pattie's questions regarding discipleship and spiritual growth and responded with awkward indifference. Her pastor told her that he had attended Princeton University, a place where he had heard very little about being born again and, to Pattie's dismay, where he had done very little serious Bible study.

God used this soul-dampening experience to ignite a passion for biblical studies in Pattie's heart. She refused to starve for lack of spiritual nourishment, so she attended a community Bible study and forged meaningful relationships with other believers. Pattie and Paul moved to Minnesota in 1975, Chicago in 1988, and back to Minnesota in 1997. Though they had attended faithful, Bible-preaching churches throughout their journeys, their second return to Minnesota planted them firmly under the preaching ministry of John Piper at Bethlehem Baptist Church in downtown Minneapolis. Pattie devoured the expository preaching of God's Word (nearly nine years through the Book of Romans) and served in the church's women's ministry. Now that she attends Redeemer Bible Church, she "continues to long for more of Jesus, to understand his call for me as I grow older." Looking back over the trials and triumphs in her life, Pattie succinctly describes it this way: "A giant trial, a giant God!" It is her God-shaped vision of life that fuels her contagiously effervescent spirit. Pattie experienced the grace of the gospel, and her life has overflowed with joy ever since.

ADVICE TO YOUNGER READERS: Trust God and his Word. Have Christian friends to support you, pray for and with you, to hold you accountable, and to have fun with!

FAVORITE PASSAGE: "Trust in the Lord with all your heart, and do not lean on your own understanding. In all your ways acknowledge him, and he will make straight your paths" (Prov. 3:5-6).

DAY 7

JANET (B. 1950)

CAPTURED BY KINDNESS

It is interesting to note that the primary text used to support the idea of Christian apologetics (i.e., defending the faith) is couched in the context of personal suffering: “But even if you should suffer for righteousness’ sake, you will be blessed. Have no fear of them, nor be troubled, but in your hearts honor Christ the Lord as holy, always being prepared to make a defense to anyone who asks you for a reason for the hope that is in you; yet do it with gentleness and respect” (1 Pet. 3:14-15). Did you notice what Peter said? As Christians display the character and grace of Christ, onlookers may be moved to ask them for an explanation, a reason for their life-sustaining hope. This is precisely what happened in Janet’s life.

Janet was born into a loving household. On Sundays, her father would take Janet, her mother, and her siblings to a nearby church. She nursed a gnawing sense of guilt when, in her seventh-grade year, her family moved to Minneapolis and stopped attending church. Added to her personal guilt was a burden she would bear much of her adolescent life—bullying. In her own words, Janet offers this terse and painful assessment: “My junior high and high school years were very lonely.” She hoped that attending college would proffer more opportunities to be accepted and make friends, but to no avail. Janet was, yet again, lonely and miserable. Yet, God's kindness met her in the valley of despair. In her Freshman English class, an assignment was given in which the students were asked to write a paper on the person who had the greatest influence in their lives. With genuine curiosity, Janet timidly asked some nearby girls the topic of their papers, and they responded, "Jesus Christ." Janet's response echoes Peter's words concerning the power of Christian living: "[Knowing they would write about Jesus] pricked my curiosity, and I began to watch their lives. They were kind to me." The girl who had grown accustomed to mockery had been captured by kindness.

It was an easy decision for Janet when these kindhearted girls invited her to attend a Christian meeting. As necessary as the girls were in God's plan for Janet's life, it was the message she heard at that meeting that changed everything. In clear, unvarnished fashion, Janet heard the gospel of Jesus Christ: "I was told God loved me, man is sinful and separated from God, Jesus Christ is God's only provision for man's sin, and we must individually receive Jesus Christ as Savior and Lord." Like Lydia by the riverside (Acts 16), the Holy Spirit opened Janet's heart to receive the gospel. The good news of outcasts being redeemed, adopted, and brought near to a loving God resonated deeply with Janet. No longer an outcast, she reveled in her new identity as a beloved daughter of the King. Her own candid assessment of her life bears repeating: "I had accepted the bullying as normal, and it wasn't until the unconditional love of those college girls and their faith in Christ that I learned differently."

Janet had been captured by kindness. Not only had the kindness of her classmates seized her attention, the kindness of a sin-forgiving, death-conquering, rebel-loving Savior had captured her heart. Janet has remained single her entire life, and she thanks God for his sustaining grace and loving presence. She continues to thank God for a loving and supportive family who stood by her through the painful years of adolescence. She praises God for granting her the grace to respond with love when treated poorly by others. In a unique way, Janet has become acquainted with the words of her Master: "Blessed are you when others revile you and persecute you and utter all kinds of evil against you falsely on my account. Rejoice and be glad, for your reward is great in heaven, for so they persecuted the prophets who were before you" (Matt. 5:11-12). The blessedness of knowing Christ and the forgiveness he alone can give has sustained Janet throughout her adult life. What began with simple acts of kindness and courtesy has blossomed into a God-honoring life of enduring grace.

ADVICE TO YOUNGER READERS: Keep focused on the fact that God is in control; meditate on his promises. Serve and witness wherever God has placed you, and guard your heart from being distracted with this world and all its false promises.

FAVORITE PASSAGE: "As it is written, 'For your sake we are being killed all the day long; we are regarded as sheep to be slaughtered.' No, in all these things we are more than conquerors through him who loved us. For I am sure that neither death nor life, nor angels nor rulers, nor things present nor things to come, nor powers, nor height nor depth, nor anything else in all creation, will be able to separate us from the love of God in Christ Jesus our Lord" (Rom. 8:36-39).

DAY 8

AL (B. 1940)

LEARNING TO KISS THE WAVES

Suicide, murder, and depression are not words that you would associate with Al. His beaming smile and endearing blue eyes would never betray the years of pain that Al has endured. Yet, his is a sober joy, one tempered by waves of heart-wrenching loss mingled with the exhilarating highs of being carried aloft on God's merciful wings. And he has a great laugh, to boot. In short, Al is a man who blesses many by osmosis, by simply being present and eagerly engaged in the moment. Born and raised in rural Spooner, Wisconsin, Al enjoyed a loving family and peaceful home life. His parents were regular church goers, but remained unconverted until later in their lives, two additional trophies of God's enduring grace.

In 1961, the twenty-one-year-old Al married a committed Roman Catholic girl. They remained in that communion until their divorce in 1973. The first wave of pain splashed upon Al's shoreline. The perennially joyful man was, for the first time in his life, brought to the yawning precipice of insanity. Al courted the unthinkable—suicide. Grace prevailed and the grave, for Al, was robbed of its prey. The merciful arm of the Lord reached down and rescued him in 1982. While attending a non-denominational Christian service, God saved Al. The glorious reality that the apostle Paul spoke about erupted in his heart: "For God, who said, 'Let light shine out of darkness,' has shone in our hearts to give the light of the knowledge of the glory of God in the face of Jesus Christ" (2 Cor. 4:6). Yet, grace was not done with the now forty-two-year-old man from Spooner. That same year he met and married Doris, the woman who would stay by his side and help him raise the son who was the glad fruit of his first marriage. Al and Doris attended various churches through the years; Al served in many roles (e.g., trustee, pastoral search team, church finance committee, facilitator of the senior's ministry, etc.). In 1993, he was baptized by immersion, an act that served as a public declaration of Al's love for and allegiance to the Lord Jesus Christ (Rom. 6:1-4).

The second wave of heartache splashed upon Al's shoreline when his eighteen-year-old son, Timothy, was murdered. The investigation that ensued found that Timothy was killed by his close friend, a reality that compounded Al's grief. With its trademark heartless timing, the siren call of alcohol lured Al into its snare with the false hopes of security, comfort, and control. Yet, the two most powerful words in Scripture broke into Al's sadness with redeeming power: *but God* (Eph. 2:4). Through the ordinary means of grace (e.g., Bible study, fellowship with other believers, and prayer), the Savior who began a good work in Al continued to guard his faltering faith. Not only did God protect Al from the eager claws of alcoholism, but he also displayed the power of his gospel in an unusually powerful way. As the homicide investigation churned on, Al became aware of the likely identity of his son's killer. Having tasted the sweetness of undeserved mercy himself, Al reached out to the young man and invited him to Bible study. The two unlikely study partners, a grieving father and his son's killer, sat together before an open Bible. If ever a saint pondered what the heavenly reunion between young Stephen and Saul might look like, here was an apt portrayal. As the Spirit of God through the Word of God worked on the heart of the young man, he eventually confessed his crime to the police and was duly arrested. Despite his grief, Al knew all too well that gloating was not option. Rather, he thanked God for earthly justice being rendered and pleaded with the Lord to pour out divine justice on Christ rather than his young Bible study partner (2 Cor. 5:21).

The third wave of unwelcome suffering rolled onto Al's weathered shoreline when his beloved wife, Doris, was diagnosed with Alzheimer's disease. The abrupt loss of a son at the hands of a killer is different than the agonizing slowness of watching one's spouse fade away. Doris was placed in a nursing home so that she could receive care and supervision, and Al lives in an apartment nearby. Although Doris does not always recognize her beloved husband, he visits her daily and prays for her to receive comfort and strength. It is little wonder that Al often quotes the Prince of Preachers, Charles Spurgeon, when he says: "Kiss the wave that throws you against the Rock of salvation."

ADVICE TO YOUNGER READERS: Men should take the lead in their homes by letting the love of Christ flow through him to his wife and kids. Young Christians should be alert to the temptation of suicide; depression and sin can take you places you never thought you would go. The Devil can smell blood when a lamb is wounded. Also, give it time and, by God's grace, things will usually change.

FAVORITE PASSAGE: "He who dwells in the shelter of the Most High will abide in the shadow of the Almighty" (Ps. 91:1).

DAY 9

BILL (B. 1954)

WHEN GOOD ISN'T GOOD ENOUGH

For a nauseating myriad of people throughout the post-Christian world, *be good for goodness' sake* is the sum of their theology. Like many young men in his generation, Bill grew up in a family that regularly attended church. Yet, in his estimation, there was "little spiritual life" in their home. With the clarity that only hindsight gives, Bill notes: "God was very real to me. I wanted to know [God] and be pleasing to him. My church and Sunday school did a fairly good job of teaching me the facts of Christianity, but I felt I had to be *good* to gain heaven." Young Bill needed to hear weighty words of the apostle Paul: "For by works of the law no human being will be justified in his sight, since through the law comes knowledge of sin" (Rom. 3:20). Even doe-eyed, well-intentioned young men like Bill cannot fulfill the unyielding demands of God's holy law. With stunning clarity, Bill describes the spiritual condition of his youth:

> I didn't know how to know God. I tried several times to read the Bible, but could never stick with it for more than a few days. On the outside I was a good person and most thought of me as such. But I knew inside that I did a good job of hiding the bad things I did and thought.

It was the provocative utterance of his tenth-grade Sunday school teacher that God used to grab the attention of the convicted and embattled young Bill. With unwavering confidence in the promises of the gospel, the teacher declared to his class that he knew, without a shadow of a doubt, that he would one day make it to heaven. The assurance that Bill craved finally seemed within reach of his weary arms.

The Savior who lived the life that Bill could never live and who died the death that Bill deserved came into focus with every page of Scripture that the young man read. The Bible that once frustrated him now thrilled him. More than two years of intense Bible reading and joyful Christian fellowship passed, and Bill came to a settled, saving knowledge of the Lord Jesus Christ. The words of the psalmist capture Bill's experience: "Your testimonies are wonderful; therefore my soul keeps them. The unfolding of your words gives light; it imparts understanding to the simple" (Ps. 119:129-130). Page after page declared the same glorious message to his tender heart: man's good is never good enough. The righteousness Bill needed to enter heaven is a righteousness granted by a merciful God who sent his Son to be the substitute for sinners like Bill (Jn. 3:16; Rom. 8:1-4).

God's kindness toward Bill took on new meaning when he married his beloved Paula. Their mutual love of the Savior sweetens the everyday pleasures of life. From browsing antique shows to reading books together, Bill and Paula rest in the knowledge that whether one eats or drinks, all can and should be done to the glory of God (1 Cor. 10:31). Yet, Bill has leaned upon the never-failing arms of the Lord when the winds of adversity threatened to topple him. In 1992, he was let go from a job he had enjoyed for 15 years, a blow that gave way to eight weeks of unemployment and uncertainty. God brought Bill back into meaningful employment, and he later learned that the company that let him go had fallen into disrepute and internal difficulties. The Lord who feeds the sparrows never failed to provide for Bill and his family.

Once a young boy who wanted to earn his way to heaven on the merits of his good behavior, Bill came to rejoice in the twin realities of his unworthiness and God's grace. Even when conflict came by way of a ministry where he loved to serve, Bill found the goodness of God operating in his life which enabled him to trust God and to show mercy as one who had received mercy from Christ. The friends he made through Campus Crusade at the University of Minnesota helped him find a healthy local church. Bill has served faithfully at Redeemer Bible Church ever since, where he delights to tell the coming generations what he needed to hear as a boy: our good isn't good enough, but through repentance and faith we can find a friend in the Good Shepherd.

ADVICE TO YOUNGER READERS: Make sure you prioritize the spiritual disciplines in your life (e.g., Bible study, prayer, fellowship, etc.). Although salvation is a free gift of God's grace through faith in Christ, there are no shortcuts in sanctification.

FAVORITE PASSAGE: "Paul, a servant of Christ Jesus, called to be an apostle, set apart for the gospel of God, which he promised beforehand through his prophets in the holy Scriptures, concerning his Son, who was descended from David according to the flesh and was declared to be the Son of God in power according to the Spirit of holiness by his resurrection from the dead, Jesus Christ our Lord" (Rom. 1:1-4).

DAY 10

DEBBIE (B. 1950)

THE WORK OF THE WORD

It seems that everyone loves a stunning testimony, one in which a person is raised from the ashes of addiction to the heights of salvation in an instant. God often does such things in order to magnify his power, grace, and mercy. However, a robust understanding of the doctrine of *regeneration* should cause us to reconsider the profundity of those testimonies that we are tempted to deem as ordinary or, heaven forbid, boring. Though there are many mysterious and unfathomable truths in God's Word, Scripture is clear when it comes to the doctrine of regeneration (i.e., what it means to be saved, born again):

> And you were dead in the trespasses and sins in which you once walked, following the course of this world, following the prince of the power of the air, the spirit that is now at work in the sons of disobedience—among whom we all once lived in the passions of our flesh, carrying out the desires of the body and the mind, and were by nature children of wrath, like the rest of mankind. But God, being rich in mercy, because of the great love with which he loved us, even when we were dead in our trespasses, made us alive together with Christ—by grace you have been saved (Eph. 2:1-5).

Debbie's salvation was a miracle. In God's mercy, he worked through his Word to cause her to be born anew at a tender age. Her testimony is as glorious as any other. Her description captures the essence of many prayers that are prayed by earnest Christian parents: "I heard the gospel proclaimed regularly and [I] do not remember a time in my life when I did not love the Lord or did not believe that he loved me and died for my sins." Debbie's young faith, as time has proven, was the work of the Word.

In Debbie's college years, she met a group of zealous young Christians. She found the fellowship she craved with other young adults who hungered for the meat of God's Word. Like miners in search of gold, they sifted through various resources (e.g., sermons, books, studies, etc.) to find faithful teachers who taught expositionally through Scripture. In the midst of this glorious season of growth, God blessed Debbie with a husband. She and Jim began attending what would later be called Redeemer Bible Church. Through the decades, Debbie and Jim have relished Christ-centered, Word-saturated fellowship that has, in her own words, caused them to "treasure his Word." It is Debbie's trust in God's Word that has stabilized her through seasons of hardship.

Within a short period of time, an unholy trinity of trials entered Debbie's life: her own cancer diagnosis, the death of her beloved mother, and Jim's brain surgery. In accordance with the Bible-based rhythm of her life, Debbie pointed to Scripture as her counsel amid pain and loss: "Count it all joy, my brothers, when you meet trials of various kinds, for you know that the testing of your faith produces steadfastness. And let steadfastness have its full effect, that you may be perfect and complete, lacking in nothing" (Jas. 1:2-4). In wonderfully visceral ways, the work of the Word continued in her life. The enduring grace of God flowed from every page of Scripture, giving rest to her soul. Looking back on this acutely difficult time in her life, Debbie notes: "I turned to the Word of God that had been faithfully taught over the years. As I leaned on my God, I experienced the power of his promises and the sustaining reality of his lovingkindness." Like her Master, God's Word has been her food and sustenance through decades of life. Amid blessing and trial, the honey of Scripture has satisfied her soul. Like David in the wilderness, Debbie has cried, "Because your steadfast love is better than life, my lips will praise you" (Ps. 63:3).

Just as we delight to share with others what we ourselves enjoy, Debbie's love for God's Word lurches forward to the coming generations. As a kind of benediction, she says, "May the Bible-teaching ministry and the fellowship of gospel-centered believers at Redeemer Bible Church continue to grow in the knowledge and love of the Savior and be a vibrant light in this community for years to come—to the praise of his glory and grace!" Indeed, such a desire is the fruit of the marvelous work of God's Word.

ADVICE TO YOUNGER READERS: Keep seeking the Lord and rest in him. As you grow in your knowledge of his Word, you will also learn not to sweat the small stuff in life.

FAVORITE PASSAGE: "I will bless the Lord at all times; his praise shall continually be in my mouth. My soul makes its boast in the Lord; let the humble hear and be glad. Oh, magnify the Lord with me, and let us exalt his name together!" (Ps. 34:1-3).

DAY 11

GARY (B. 1957)

THE WONDERS OF ADVERSITY

In his classic *Confessions*, Augustine wrote these immortal words: "You have made us for yourself, O Lord, and our hearts are restless until they rest in you." The words of Augustine describe Gary's experience as a young man. Baptized as an infant, he assumed he was a Christian. Attending a church that rarely spoke of God's holiness, the dangers of sin, the need for repentance, and faith in Christ alone did not help him at all. Through his youth, Gary thought that salvation depended upon "[good] works and how good a person I was." In college, he tried to satisfy the restlessness of his soul by throwing himself into academic pursuits. Obtaining a perfect GPA held out the promise of joy, and a high-paying job seemed like a noble pursuit for any ambitious young man. Yet, Gary's own words betray the vanity of setting one's affections on earthly attainments: "I made it through my senior year, but I continued to have this gnawing emptiness as to what I was doing." Truly, our hearts are restless until...

In God's kind providence, Gary was invited by his sister-in-law to attend her church. It was a modest Baptist congregation that preached the gospel and honored the authority of God's Word. Gary agreed to attend and listened as the preacher exposited the Book of Ecclesiastes, a book that highlights the vanity of life's pursuits apart from seeking God's glory. Indeed, this proved to be a turning point in Gary's life as Ecclesiastes ministered to his restless and dissatisfied soul. Through the preaching of Scripture and the loving mentorship of other believers, Gary repented of his sin and threw himself into the arms of Jesus Christ. The Bread of Life satiated his desires, and Gary began feasting on Bible study materials, sermons, and commentaries. The more of Christ's glory that Gary saw, the more settled his soul became. Reflecting on that season of his life, he says: "Through his Word, which is very important to me, he has helped me to see the need to fear him, seek him, to see his love, and the extent he wants me to follow him." Restless no more, Gary set his eyes on marriage, service in his local church, and parenthood.

Gary's firm foundation in the gospel of God's grace prepared him for the many trials that would come into his life. Alongside his loving wife, he has been called to shepherd his family and the unique challenges that fatherhood brings. He thanks God for his wife's care for their girls as she takes them to doctor appointments and ensures they receive proper care and education. He glowingly affirms that "she definitely resembles the woman who fears the Lord in Proverbs 31." God has continued to strengthen Gary as a father and a husband, roles that delight him greatly.

Recently, Gary has struggled with various health issues. The painful yet hope-filled truth from the apostle Paul echoes throughout Gary's life: "So we do not lose heart. Though our outer self is wasting away, our inner self is being renewed day by day" (2 Cor. 4:16). As he trusts God for sustaining grace in his own health battles, he is also serving his elderly parents. Gary's mother was placed in a nursing home after suffering from a stroke, and Gary's father wanted to be with her. Gary and his family made arrangements for his parents, and he continues to serve them by bringing supplies, medications, and a much-needed smile. Gary says it best when he comments on his life: "Jesus has shown me his love through trials, reminding me that he paid a very steep penalty for my sins on the cross and that he saved a sinner like me. God works great wonders through adversity and trials." The once restless college student has become a content servant to his friends and family—all because of God's enduring grace in Christ Jesus.

ADVICE TO YOUNGER READERS: Be in God's Word as much as possible and pray without ceasing. Persevere when trials, hardships, and difficulties arise. Wait on the Lord and stay in his Word. It can be incredibly hard to do this since we often assume that God is against us in those dark seasons. That is why his Word, the promises of the gospel, and the community of faith are so incredibly important.

FAVORITE PASSAGE: "Though the fig tree should not blossom, nor fruit be on the vines, the produce of the olive fail and the fields yield no food, the flock be cut off from the fold and there be no herd in the stalls, yet I will rejoice in the Lord; I will take joy in the God of my salvation. God, the Lord, is my strength; he makes my feet like the deer's; he makes me tread on my high places" (Hab. 3:17-19).

DAY 12

JIM (B. 1936)

ALL OF GRACE

The picture of a young boy, in the early 1940's, sitting on his beloved father's lap listening to him explain the gospel is glorious and heartwarming. This scene is more than an idea or sentiment; it is precisely what took place in Jim's childhood. Reminiscing on that period of his youth, Jim states: "He [father] explained that Jesus died to pay the price for my sins and that he rose from the dead. At the time I knew that sassing mom and spitting on the sidewalk were sins, but I came to realize that the sins I had committed are far greater but still forgiven." God's grace came to Jim at an early age and remained with him as he went on to attend college and serve in the U.S. Army. Yet, upon returning home from his military service, Jim realized that he was spiritually famished. He wanted the meat of God's Word, and he began searching for it.

The Lord rewarded Jim's desire by bringing Don and Marlene George into his life. At a weekly lunch that the George's served in their home, Jim learned about the church they attended. He was intrigued: "I learned that the church they attended, Maranatha Bible Church (now Redeemer Bible Church), taught the Word of God in context." Jim not only wanted biblically oriented teaching, but he also wanted biblical teaching that handled God's Word with integrity and care. It was also in this period of the early 1970's that Jim attended a Bible study with other zealous young adults. In addition to finding sweet fellowship with other believers, he also met "a young lady with a wise, searching mind and soul," a lady who would become his wife. Jim and his beloved wife have attended Redeemer Bible Church ever since, and those decades of expository, gospel-centered preaching have provided Jim with a sturdy foundation and a tender heart. The excellence in teaching Scripture that Jim craves has been driven by a desire to see the grace of God in Christ magnified. Such a cross-shaped vision for life has sustained Jim through many hardships. The psalmist's words reverberate throughout Jim's life: "Consider how I love your precepts! Give me life according to your steadfast love" (Ps. 119:159).

As the Word of God crept more deeply into Jim's bloodstream, he was being prepared to face a significant trial of life and faith. Shortly after his 70th birthday, vision problems revealed a more threatening issue in Jim's life—a brain tumor. Despite a successful initial surgery, numerous complications arose including Myasthenia gravis, blood clots in his lungs, a perforated colon, and excessive internal bleeding. Jim looks back on this season of his life and joyfully recounts that he "experienced God's sustaining grace in providing peace and just the right people at the right time." It is easy to understand how a man could face so many physical maladies with joy and hope. Being filled with Scripture, Jim experienced what Paul prescribed for the Philippian Christians: "Do not be anxious about anything, but in everything by prayer and supplication with thanksgiving let your requests be made known to God. And the peace of God, which surpasses all understanding, will guard your hearts and your minds in Christ Jesus" (Phil. 4:6-7). Although their souls are secure in Christ, many believers face unique forms of suffering as they grow older, and Jim is no exception.

Yet, amid pain and fear, Christians like Jim also experience greater depths of God's grace. As their bodies fail, they realize that their hope is not contingent upon their strength or even their ability to serve their Lord. It is all of Christ; it is all of grace. Jim makes this point clear: "While the times have not been without physical or financial challenges, I praise God for his faithfulness and for the assurance that comes from Scripture. As in Ephesians

2:8-9, the grace and faith in God for salvation are gifts from God and are not dependent upon what I do." Jim has faced many hardships with buoyant and unsinkable joy because the promises of God's Word have embedded themselves into his DNA. From a tender conversation on his father's lap to an operating table, God's enduring grace has sustained Jim through decades of faithful service to his Lord. Jim remains jealous for others to know that it is all because of grace.

ADVICE TO YOUNGER READERS: Take time to be in God's Word and prayer every day and seek out a church that keeps God's Word at the center of its preaching and teaching.

FAVORITE PASSAGE: "For by grace you have been saved through faith. And this is not your own doing; it is the gift of God, not a result of works, so that no one may boast" (Eph. 2:8-9).

DAY 13

ED (B. 1957)

ANXIOUS BUT ANCHORED

It takes a volatile mixture of pain and wisdom to confess that one's primary issue in life is pride. Admitting to working too much, caring too much, or trying too hard are often subterfuges to protect the citadel of self. Yet, God's grace has brought Ed to such a place, one of self-effacing wisdom. He grew up in a Roman Catholic household and was confirmed at age 13, but the concept of grace eluded him. Ed looks back and notes: "I thought salvation was by works, and I pictured myself climbing a ladder to heaven. For every good deed I did, I would go up one step. For every bad thing I did, I would slip down one rung." In his teens, Ed found himself groping for meaning. He looks back and notes, "I was haunted by the meaninglessness of life and tried to find it in books, music, sports, and even the world of the occult." Yet, Ed came to understand the potency of two of Scripture's sweetest words: *But God...*

A glorious chain reaction took place in Ed's family as his sister became a Christian while at college. She shared the gospel with their other sister who then became a Christian also. God's grace was sweeping through their home and was headed straight for Ed. In the summer of 1973, Ed's sister shared the gospel with him. He notes: "I can remember that as she read the verses of Scripture, especially Romans, it was as if a light was coming into my heart...

The biggest change for me in the days following my conversion was a hunger for God's Word and a peace and joy that I had never experienced before." The anxious teen who sought peace in the dark corners of spiritualism found it by being captured by the Light of the World, Jesus Christ (2 Cor. 4:6).

Over forty years have passed since the Lord opened Ed's heart to receive the gospel of grace. Since then, his spiritual growth has continued, but not without its ups and downs. After graduating from college, Ed spent ten years working as a landscape architect before stepping out in faith and enlisting in a Bible translation effort that would take him across the globe. His love of God's Word propelled him to bring the Scriptures to unreached people of India and Nepal. Although he relished his assignment in the mission field, Ed was thrust into a season of intense stress in 1993. However, God graciously worked through Ed's pain to bring about fruit: "Dealing with this suffering led me to Reformed writers such as R. C. Sproul, Jerry Bridges, and J. I. Packer...The Reformed take on the sovereignty of God was like spiritual ballast for my soul." Although his battle with anxiety and worry remains a theme in his life, Ed presses on with the hope that the God who started a good work in him will undoubtedly bring it to completion (Phil. 1:6).

One of the greatest means of grace in Ed's life came when he was 39. He was blessed with a beautiful, godly wife who gladly served alongside him in the Bible translation and mission efforts. Ed rejoices over God's kindness by stating, "We have enjoyed a full life of sweet, compatible friendship and love." Ed and his bride have seen God prove himself faithful time and again in their years of marriage and Christian service. Notably, his translation work in the New Testament was completed in Nepal in 2018. After one of the local pastors read from Luke's Gospel and the Parable of the Prodigal Son, one of his hearers came to embrace Christ as Lord and Savior. Ed maintains that this incident is one of the highlights of his translation work.

Ed's work continues in Nepal, and though he loves serving his Master, he continues to battle anxiety. Yet, he faces each day with hope since he is no longer adrift in a sea of undefined spiritualism;

he is anchored by the Rock of Ages. In his fight against anxiety, Ed has learned the following: "The sanctification project continues, but with a deeper, wider foundation and a growing abandonment of outcomes that I cannot or should not try to control." Through God's enduring grace, the once anxious young man now finds his rest by being anchored in Christ.

ADVICE TO YOUNGER READERS: Remember the words of Annie Dillard: *How we spend our days is how we spend our lives.* In Matthew 6, Jesus says that even though there are legitimate things with which we are to concern ourselves, the one thing we are to prioritize above all else is seeking him (Matt. 6:33). So, don't let life overshadow your concern for eternal life. Seeking the Lord and his kingdom are not means of earning salvation; they are calls to enjoy him!

FAVORITE PASSAGE: "O Lord, my heart is not lifted up; my eyes are not raised too high; I do not occupy myself with things too great and too marvelous for me. But I have calmed and quieted my soul, like a weaned child with its mother; like a weaned child is my soul within me. O Israel, hope in the Lord from this time forth and forevermore" (Ps. 131:1-3).

DAY 14

JUDY (B. 1950)

THE GENTLE HAND OF GOD

For many Americans, coming of age in the volatile 1960's was hard, disorienting, and scarring. Judy was no exception. Her worldview was shaped by feminism and unfettered personal freedom. Looking back on those tender years, Judy describes herself with a single, jarring adjective: *horrible*. Yet, God's enduring grace outran Judy's rebellion. At the age of 48, he claimed her as a trophy of grace and opened her eyes to the supremacy and beauty of Jesus Christ. In his trademark fashion, God used the foolish things of the world to shame the wise. Judy was invited to a neighbor's house to celebrate her daughter's 11th birthday. After the celebration, the little girl handed a book to Judy and asked her to read it to her. It was a child's book about heaven and how to get there. The seed of curiosity was planted in Judy's mind, and she sought out more mature Christian literature. Through her personal studies, Judy gave her life to Christ. After excitedly announcing the news to her neighbor, the mother of 12 children committed to meeting with Judy at 5:30am to disciple the middle-aged convert. Judy's husband was not a believer, so her infant years as a Christian were once marked by duplicity as she aimed to honor her husband while also honoring her Lord. With the help of her sister, Judy eventually started attending Redeemer Bible Church and relished the expository preaching of

God's Word. The feminist was now a humble and happy member of the bride of Christ.

As with so many of God's people, the winds of adversity roared into Judy's life. At age 52, her husband developed Alzheimer's disease, and Judy became his sole caregiver. She gladly served her husband for nearly four years until home health assistants stepped in to help provide care. This allowed Judy to reengage in church life and regain deep relationships with members of her small group. These would prove to be crucial means of grace in her life as her husband, Dave, passed away in 2009 after a long seven-year battle with the crippling disease. Nevertheless, God's grace continued to carry Judy. She attended a Tuesday women's Bible study where she dove deeper into the riches of the gospel. Learning that Christ took her place under God's wrath caused Judy's heart to swell with gratitude for her Savior. Yet, she also notes that God was "a true gentleman…he exposed my sin little by little. If it had washed over me all at once, the devastation would have been too great." God's firm but gentle hand led Judy into sweet communion with Christ and a richer understanding of his love for her.

The gentle hand of the Good Shepherd remained on Judy's shoulder as she walked through more trials. The summer after Judy was saved, she sought to reconnect with the daughter she gave up for adoption many years ago. By God's grace, she was able to find her and, over time, develop a sweet relationship with her. Though she remains grateful for the reconciliation she experienced with her daughter, Sharyn, it made her daughter's death a bitter providence indeed. Judy's faith continued to be tested as she received a colon cancer diagnosis. A friend from church was a nurse, and she accompanied Judy to her appointments to offer Christ-centered encouragement to the nervous widow. Despite the anxiety that cancer often brings, Judy says that "God's grace was obvious to me through his comfort and his people." The gentle hand of providence led Judy through the valley of the shadow of death, and she emerged with a song of praise in her heart.

Before her husband's death, Judy was able to share the gospel with him. The Alzheimer's had yet to ravish all of Dave's cognitive abilities, and Judy seized the opportunity to tell him about God, sin, Christ, and his need for repentance and faith. As his disease progressed, one night Judy was awakened by the sound of Dave crying out, "Jesus! Jesus! Jesus!" She finds solace in being able to place her husband's frail hand into the nail-pierced hands of their Savior. These and many other instances of suffering in Judy's life have been buoyed by this promise: "Fear not, for I am with you; be not dismayed, for I am your God; I will strengthen you, I will help you, I will uphold you with my righteous right hand" (Isa. 41:10). As a young feminist, Judy raised a clinched fist of defiance to God, but his grace and his gentle hand won her over.

ADVICE TO YOUNGER READERS: Pray and ask the Lord to put godly people in your life, people who are willing to lovingly speak his truth to you. Also, zealously guard your heart against friendships that would pull you away from the Lord Jesus.

FAVORITE PASSAGE: "And I am sure of this, that he who began a good work in you will bring it to completion at the day of Jesus Christ" (Phil. 1:6).

DAY 15

KATHY (B. 1950)

FROM MILK TO MEAT

Everyone loves a dramatic testimony. A young heroin addict reads a gospel tract that thcy found on the sidewalk and experiences a glorious and powerful transformation. A dying alcoholic who refused to attend church all his life weeps at hearing the gospel on his deathbed. Such stories are wonderful and God-honoring. Yet, for many of God's people, the light of the gospel shines brightly and early in their lives. Kathy is one such person. Her words should prove to be wise counsel and comfort for others who, by God's sovereign grace, are saved at a young age: "I used to wish I had a more dramatic testimony like the apostle Paul and so many others. But, as I matured in my faith, I came to the realization that it was a glorious gift being raised in a Baptist church by believing parents and with excellent Sunday school teachers and youth leaders."

Kathy was baptized by immersion at the age of 12 and, despite being a sinner in daily need of the gospel's power, she felt the presence of Christ throughout her youth. By God's grace and the help other faithful Christians speaking into her life, she was constantly reminded of the truth of 2 Corinthians 5:21, a verse that many theologians lovingly refer to as The Great Exchange: "For our sake he made him to be sin who knew no sin, so that in him we might become the righteousness of God." The truth of Christ's substitutionary death, powerful resurrection from the dead, and his victorious ascension to the right hand of God galvanized Kathy's faith amid the ups and downs of adolescence. As she dug deeper into God's Word, seeing more of Christ's refulgent glory, her hunger for spiritual nourishment strengthened. Kathy notes: "As my diet from milk to meat increased, my love for the Lord increased exponentially as well as my desire to live for the cause of Christ without reservation." Kathy's testimony is a resounding example of how grace propels obedience, how seeing the beauty of Christ fuels living for the honor of Christ.

Kathy met and married a wonderful, godly man named Rich. The Lord blessed them with three sons, and two of them were called upon to serve in active military combat service in Iraq. After they attended the historic West Point training academy, the young men were well-equipped for their 22-month deployment into active warfare. Their doting mother, Kathy, was also prepared for a time of battle. As the boys boarded the plane to depart for the other side of the world, Kathy entered her own war against anxiety, fear, and stress. Her years spent meditating upon, studying, and memorizing God's Word proved to be adequate weapons for the fight. Rich and Kathy experienced the grace and peace of God throughout this season of their lives through their own times of prayer as well as through the prayers of beloved friends and family. Both of their sons returned from battle unharmed, each receiving awards including the Bronze Star and the coveted Purple Heart.

Another highlight of Kathy's life was serving as a teaching leader for women's and young adult Bible studies. For 11 years, she poured herself into other women, laboring to help them see the glory of Christ in all of Scripture and to hold God's Word in its rightful place of authority. The Lord sweetened Kathy's experience by allowing her to serve alongside her husband, Rich. Both marvel as they recount God's faithfulness and blessing through their years of ministry work. Seeing God's grace in the lives of others who, by way of Kathy and Rich's tutelage, went on to be leaders themselves continues to give them deep and abiding joy. Not only has she seen other leaders raised up, but she has also had the pleasure of seeing many of her students find and marry godly spouses. She has come to know something of Paul's delight in the Thessalonians: "For what is our hope or joy or crown of boasting before our Lord Jesus at his coming? Is it not you? For you are our glory and joy" (1 Thess. 2:19-20).

For the young, milk is an ideal source of nourishment. For the hungry soul, however, only spiritual meat will truly satisfy. God graciously ignited an appetite in Kathy's soul at an early age, and she has been savoring the food of his Word ever since. If we affirm the teaching of Scripture concerning the spiritual deadness of fallen man (Eph. 2:1-3), we come to see testimonies like Kathy's for what they truly are—miracles.

ADVICE TO YOUNGER READERS: Your spouse simply must come first. Although children, careers, and ministry opportunities are important, you must be intentional about prioritizing your spouse among the other demands you are called to steward.

FAVORITE PASSAGE: "In him we have obtained an inheritance, having been predestined according to the purpose of him who works all things according to the counsel of his will, so that we who were the first to hope in Christ might be to the praise of his glory" (Eph. 1:11-12).

DAY 16

DEE DEE (B. 1959)

SEARCHING FOR THE TRUTH, FOUND BY THE SAVIOR

A little girl with dark hair sits at a wooden desk, her tennis shoes barely touching the tile floor. Despite the presence of other young students in the musty school room, the silence is palpable. The girl's parents have labored to instill good morals and a strong work ethic in her. Perhaps this is why her #2 pencil shakes as the adrenaline courses through her veins. Some of the questions on the exam are painfully unfamiliar. This should not be the case; she studied so hard. Yet, the exam's demands for perfect answers continue to bully her. In desperation, the girl did what her stalwart father taught her to do in times of trouble—she prayed to the spirit of her deceased grandmother and implored her for help. Dee Dee begged her revered grandmother to grant her a blessing so that she could pass her test and bring honor to her family. Growing up in Hong Kong, such a practice was common. Dee Dee had Christian acquaintances in high school, but none of them shared their faith explicitly with her. So, she remained at the mercy of deceased relatives for the help she desperately needed.

In 1988, Dee Dee married an American man named Carl. Although she was not a Christian at the time, it was still very important for her to be married in a church. The couple received premarital counseling, but the truth she wanted to know yet again eluded her. The minister proved to be a hireling who failed to unfold the glory of the gospel of Christ for them. Even when her husband's job brought them to Singapore, Dee Dee continued searching for a church that would tell her the truth of Scripture. Although she attended a few churches in Singapore, none of them sufficed. She resigned herself to live by her own rules. Eventually, Dee Dee and Carl moved to Minnesota where, by God's grace, they found a church that preached Scripture. While attending a small group, Dee Dee was able to submit her gnawing questions about God, Scripture, Christ, salvation, and myriad other matters. Mercifully, her group members supplied biblically faithful answers, and, in time, Dee Dee joyfully submitted to the Lord's command to be baptized. She slowly began to realize that her search for truth was birthed and sustained by the One seeking her: "No one can come to me unless the Father who sent me draws him. And I will raise him up on the last day" (Jn. 6:44).

The Lord blessed Dee Dee and Carl with two children. Though she loved being a mother, she also came to realize how God uses children to discipline and sanctify his (adult) children. Always the strong, disciplined type, Dee Dee leaned into the pressures of parenthood with grit and determination. Laudable attributes such as these, when they are devoid of God's grace, become millstones around one's neck. Yet, the Good Shepherd disciplines his sheep in a spirit of love and gentleness. The writer of Hebrews makes this point unequivocally clear: "For the moment all discipline seems painful rather than pleasant, but later it yields the peaceful fruit of righteousness to those who have been trained by it" (Heb. 12:11). God used her children to teach Dee Dee about her need of grace in *every* area of her life. From difficult exams to teething babies, God's enduring grace abides with his needy people.

Not only did God's grace abound to her amid the joys and trials of parenthood, but the Lord also protected Dee Dee and her children when disaster struck. With the entire family in the car, her husband was driving southbound when they were struck from behind by another vehicle. They were launched into oncoming traffic and struck by two more vehicles. Mercifully, no one was hurt. The car was totaled, but Dee Dee and her family had not so much as a scratch. She would experience the kind hand of providence again in 2016. In the middle of the night, Dee Dee and Carl's home caught fire and was damaged beyond repair. After several years, they were finally able to rebuild and reestablish their lives. From car accidents to house fires to numerous domestic and international moves, her Savior has always proven to be faithful and kind. No longer does Dee Dee pray for blessings from deceased relatives. Now she finds daily strength to face fear and anxiety because she knows she serves a living King, one who gave his perfect life in exchange for hers and sought out his wandering sheep until he found her.

ADVICE TO YOUNGER READERS: Cling to God's Word and treasure it for what it truly is—*the* truth! Go to Bible studies with other believers and seek ways to apply Scripture to every area of your life. Be quick to repent and run to the Lord, and trust in him despite your circumstances.

FAVORITE PASSAGE: "Trust in the Lord with all your heart, and do not lean on your own understanding. In all your ways acknowledge him, and he will make straight your paths" (Prov. 3:5-6).

DAY 17

PAUL (B. 1934)

THE STRONG BONDS OF THE GOLDEN CHAIN

In Duluth, MN there is a harbor in which large freight ships can find refuge from the volatile winds and waves of Lake Superior. In order to provide stability to a ship weighing more than 100 hundred tons, large chains are needed. This proves to be an apt illustration upon which theologians through the centuries have seized to describe Paul's words in Romans 8:30. There, the apostle unabashedly declares the immovable certainty of God's plan of salvation for his people: "And those whom he predestined he also called, and those whom he called he also justified, and those whom he justified he also glorified." In order for Christians to have ballast amid storms, the golden chain of Romans 8 provides strong assurance that their God will complete the work of redemption that he began in them. Perhaps it is the strength of this verse that has produced such enduring fruit in the life of another man named Paul.

"In the summer of 1976, I committed my life to the Lordship of Jesus Christ at Northern Pines Family Camp in Lake Geneva, WI. On December 3, 1978, I was baptized by immersion...But my life before and after that reflects the sovereign hand of God in his foreknowledge, predestination, calling, justification, glorification, and sanctification through the work of the Holy Spirit and the Word. All has been by God's grace and through no merit of my own," Paul humbly yet confidently asserts. Although his father or grandfather would regularly take him to church, they rarely attended themselves. Paul was always interested in spiritual matters and even enrolled in a religion course while at college. One of the required texts for his class, *The Nature and Destiny of Man* by Reinhold Niebuhr, convinced Paul of the utter sinfulness of mankind. In graduate school, Paul joined an Episcopal church. Later, after being hired by a large company in 1958, he met and married Pattie who was also an Episcopalian. Despite their regular church involvement, the Lord had other plans for the young couple.

In 1973, Pattie joined a fellowship for Christian women where she heard the gospel of Jesus Christ with precision and clarity. Pattie was born again. For the next three years, she peppered Paul with questions about the state of his soul and whether his faith was merely intellectual. God used her loving inquiries to bring Paul to Northern Pines camp in 1976. In 1978, they left the Episcopal Church and began attending a Baptist church that preached expositorally through Scripture. Paul also committed himself to the reading of the entire Bible once per year. He has maintained this practice consistently for over 40 years. Paul's passion for God's Word was stoked into a flame as he and Pattie joined Bethlehem Baptist Church in Minneapolis, MN and sat under the preaching ministry of John Piper for many years. Paul would go on to serve as an elder at Bethlehem for 18 years. It was also during his tenure at Bethlehem that Paul became an ardent defender of Reformed theology. The truth contained in Romans 8:30 (i.e., God's sovereignty in salvation) gripped Paul's mind and heart. It would prove to be his commitment to a high view of God and his providence that would steady him during the trials to come.

In 2010, his beloved Pattie was diagnosed with breast cancer. Though God's mercy would carry her through to remission, it came at a high cost to her body. Moreover, Paul and Pattie suffered through multiple miscarriages throughout their marriage, though they were blessed with two daughters who remain committed Christians. Knowing that God controls all things and works all circumstances for the eternal good of his children, Paul was able to provide the leadership and love his wife and family needed. In his own words, Paul says: "The providence of God is good and real; it overcomes all our needs." Knowing that his life was secure in the harbor of God's grace, secured by the golden chain of redemption that his Savior bought for him, Paul persevered through many decades of faithful Christian service. Chains can be synonymous with captivity, but when a man is a slave of King Jesus, he finds them to be the robes of freedom and the garments of much praise.

ADVICE TO YOUNGER READERS: Commit as much Scripture to memory as possible and include the specific citations. Hiding God's Word in your heart and mind will prepare you for the battles to come.

FAVORITE PASSAGE: "Have I not commanded you? Be strong and courageous. Do not be frightened, and do not be dismayed, for the Lord your God is with you wherever you go" (Josh. 1:9).

DAY 18

WANDA (B. 1950)

THROUGH THE FLAMES AND ON TO GLORY

The great London preacher, Charles Haddon Spurgeon, was saved when a snowstorm forced him to slip into the back row of a small Methodist church. Soon after, the soon-to-be Prince of Preachers was baptized in the River Lark. A young law student, Martin Luther, cried out for mercy and committed himself to a life of monastic study when a lightning storm caused him to fear for his life. In 1709, the young John Wesley was saved from imminent tragedy when his family's home caught fire in the middle of the night. With the clarity that only hindsight can afford, one can clearly see God's grace at work amid altered plans, fear, and tragedy. Interestingly, many of these same elements are present in the life and testimony of a dear woman named Wanda.

"I was raised in a Christian home," Wanda says, "and I went forward at a camp meeting and put my faith in Jesus and what he did for me. I was baptized the next day in a nearby creek." Like Spurgeon, Wanda professed her love for and commitment to King Jesus in the amphitheater of nature. As her family's fifth child, Wanda's mother experienced a difficult pregnancy and was unsure if her precious baby daughter would survive infancy due to a kidney blockage. Yet, God's mercy abounded and Wanda survived. Like Luther, she battled fear through her childhood as the threat of disease and illness loomed over her life. Her community was rocked by a flu epidemic in which many babies and toddlers perished. Wanda's family kept her hydrated, provided constant care, and prayed incessantly for Wanda's young life to be spared. Graciously, it was. She also recounts: "When I was two years old, I had measles, mumps, chicken pox, and scarlet fever…I almost died." Like Wesley, her home was destroyed when lightning struck near her family farm and ignited a fire that would consumer everything that her family owned. Wanda survived, but all that was left were the pajamas she wore to bed. Despite her young age, Wanda held on to the words of the apostle Peter: "In this [your salvation] you rejoice, though now for a little while, if necessary, you have been grieved by various trials, so that the tested genuineness of your faith—more precious than gold that perishes though it is tested by fire—may be found to result in praise and glory and honor at the revelation of Jesus Christ" (1 Pet. 1:6-7).

In her early 20's Wanda struggled in her walk with Christ. Like so many young people coming of age in the tumultuous 1960's, Wanda found herself adrift in a sea of relativism. She says: "I came to a point where I could not honestly say I knew what was right and what was wrong." Such is the madness of abandoning God's authoritative revelation for the philosophies of men. Yet, the Lord lovingly corrected Wanda and brought her back under his wing. Indeed, the words of the writer to the Hebrews proved to be sweet in Wanda's life: "For the Lord disciplines the one he loves, and chastises every son whom he receives" (Heb. 12:6). She fondly recalls how God kept her from making a shipwreck of her faith: "It scared me, and I cried out to the Lord to show me what to do. I asked him to help me follow him. Within a short period of time, everything in my life changed, and I was walking a path that brought me closer to Christ." Wanda began attending what would come to be known as Redeemer Bible Church during this time, and its ministry of expository preaching strengthened her faith and helped her to see the worthiness of King Jesus.

In 2014, Wanda started her own business without having a customer base or secondary income. It was a time of trusting the Lord, praying, and taking one day at a time. Praying for our daily bread is one thing; waiting for it to arrive is quite another. However, God met all of Wanda's needs. She gladly recalls his faithfulness during those lean years: "I trusted Jesus to provide, and he did. I never missed a mortgage or bill payment; I lacked for nothing from that time until now in my retirement years." Wanda's life began with trials. From perennial illness to a raging house fire, she learned at a tender age to trust the Lord. She has come, quite literally, through the flames, and she knows her faithful Shepherd will bring her home to glory.

ADVICE TO YOUNGER READERS: Memorize a chapter in the Psalms, one that really speaks to your soul. Recite it often and let is become part of your bloodstream. Also, take to heart the lyrics of the classic hymn, *Great is Thy Faithfulness*.

FAVORITE PASSAGE: "I lift up my eyes to the hills. From where does my help come? My help comes from the Lord, who made heaven and earth. He will not let your foot be moved; he who keeps you will not slumber. Behold, he who keeps Israel will neither slumber nor sleep. The Lord is your keeper; the Lord is your shade on your right hand" (Ps. 121:1-5).

DAY 19

KATHY (B. 1943)

WHEN RELUCTANCE GIVES WAY TO REJOICING

"This is going to be awful," Kathy muttered to herself. Her aunt invited her to attend a Bible study, something that Kathy had no desire to do. She could imagine all the stone-faced, Bible-clutching women who would quietly judge her as she entered the room. No, Kathy would rather drink poison than attend a gathering like that. Yet, her beloved aunt asked her to join the group, so she begrudgingly agreed. Why would Kathy feel a desire to go? The church she grew up in as a youth never preached the gospel. Without the grace of God in Christ being a central theme to the life and preaching of a congregation, all that is left is powerless moralism and joyless adherence to laws and tradition. Kathy's heart was not moved with affection to read and study God's Word; it remained a locked book to her. At the urging of her husband, Jim, Kathy walked into the women's study only to be shocked and dismayed. She recalls: "Upon entering the sanctuary, I was surrounded by happy women!" Theirs was not a feigned or glib happiness but a real, abiding, authentic joy. Kathy was intrigued.

There she sat, riveted on the speaker's Bible lesson. Once the lecture concluded, she was invited to remain in a newcomer's class. An older woman stepped to the lectern and began explaining the gospel of Jesus Christ with clarity, precision, and compassion. Kathy recalls: "I felt suspended and as the Word of God seeped into my thoughts, I understood what the Bible was saying." It was there, at the Bible study she desperately wanted to avoid, that God's enduring grace invaded her life and opened her eyes to her need of the Savior. Naturally, Kathy wanted to share the good news with her closest friends. So, at a lunch meeting she began to recall how God had marvelously saved her at the Bible study. To her dismay, she was waved off with a yawn. Just as Kathy had been only days before, the ladies were indifferent to the gospel. No matter for Kathy. Her newfound love for Christ was undiminished and she began hunting for a new Bible. Eventually she found one that she liked, and Scripture has been her daily bread ever since.

After marrying Jim, the Lord blessed Kathy with three children. She delighted in motherhood, but soon found herself pleading with the Lord for wisdom as she and Jim decided how best to educate their kids. Kathy's preeminent concern was the salvation of her children. In her zeal, she sent her first daughter to a private school downtown. Yet, she soon realized that the school was steeped in lifeless legalism rather than the life-giving joy of the gospel. The happiness of the women that grabbed her attention earlier in life was exactly what she wanted her daughter to experience. Through the years, God guided Jim and Kathy as they sought to ground their children in the joy of the gospel. Now, many years later, all three of their children live nearby and they enjoy the laughter of great-grandchildren.

Just as she began her journey with Christ at a Bible study, God's Word has remained central to Kathy's life. The Lord's words in the desert echo throughout her life as well: "Man shall not live by bread alone, but by every word that comes from the mouth of God" (Matt. 4:4). In addition to the joy of motherhood, Kathy also rejoices over God's kindness in bringing her to faithful, healthy, Bible-preaching churches throughout her life. Rather than attractions and programs, Kathy's heart has always hungered for the meat of God's Word and the primacy of expository preaching.

By God's grace, this is precisely what she has received through the years. She cherishes his Word. The reluctant convert is now the unashamed follower of Jesus Christ. Committed to the Scriptures she once avoided, Kathy extols the words of Paul: "All Scripture is breathed out by God and profitable for teaching, for reproof, for correction, and for training in righteousness, that the man of God may be complete, equipped for every good work" (2 Tim. 3:16-17). The Bible is no longer a locked book for Kathy. Her hunger to see Christ on every page only intensifies as the years pass. Only beauty can compel such an obsession. Only that which is supremely satisfying can eclipse other desires. Only the glory of Jesus Christ can change reluctance into rejoicing.

ADVICE TO YOUNGER READERS: The fact is, we simply cannot love a God we know nothing about. In his mercy, he gave us his authoritative revelation, his Word. The Bible is living, and it will surprise you by consistently feeding you in different ways. So, feast on your Bible. Get a good study Bible and read it slowly. Don't hurry through it. Read God's Word over and over again, relishing each passage.

FAVORITE PASSAGE: "For the Word of God is living and active, sharper than any two-edged sword, piercing to the division of soul and spirit, of joints and marrow, and discerning the thoughts and intentions of the heart" (Heb. 4:12).

DAY 20

KELLY (B. 1965)

IRRESISTIBLE GRACE, INDESCRIBABLE SAVIOR

The gray moss swung in the branches of an ancient oak tree. The summer humidity caused a faint haze to hover in the air. The dog days were squarely upon the deep south, and there was no escape and little relief. The youngest of six children, Kelly found respite from the sweltering heat by riding horses at a neighbor's home. She grew up in an all-too-familiar situation in America's Bible Belt. Her family was, in her estimation, nominal/cultural Christians whose faith could best be described as a kind of sentimental deism. God was mentioned, but social status, political alliances, and comfort were the ruling gods of the day. Despite her father's success as a doctor, he remained a functional alcoholic. So, Kelly's mother took the children to church. God's grace penetrated the fog of her home life and Kelly felt a love for God and an interest in his Word at an early age. God used her neighbor to bring the light of the gospel into Kelly's dim world. One day after her usual horseback ride, Kelly enjoyed a cool glass of lemonade with the kind lady who owned the property. Looking back with fondness, Kelly recounts: "I had never met anyone who loved or knew Jesus as she did, and I was drawn irresistibly to him. One of those afternoons at the kitchen table in their old southern plantation-style home, God brought me to himself." Kelly was 12 years old, and her life would never be the same.

In her youthful zeal, Kelly announced to her family that she had been born again. Their replies could have stifled her growth: *We're all Christians, Kelly. After all, we are Americans! You don't need to be a fanatic!* Their efforts failed. By God's enduring grace, Kelly is able to say: "Happily, I never got over it and the phase never passed. Jesus is able to save completely those who come to God through him." Kelly would leave the heat of the American south for the heat of Asia where she would serve in various ministry capacities. It was on the mission field that she met her husband, Ed. She has relished the opportunity to serve alongside her husband as he labors in Bible translation work. Kelly notes: "Doing linguistic surveys in different states of northern India, Bangladesh, and Nepal meant getting to see up close and personal several of the many tribes, tongues, and nations that will worship around God's throne. Several of these languages now have New Testaments and some are starting to receive the Old Testament in their native tongue."

Though missions work overseas has enabled Kelly to witness God's blessings, she has also relied upon God's mercy amid numerous trials. The Maoist civil war in Nepal, working in hostile territory, suffering four miscarriages, loneliness, a horrific earthquake in 2015, and perennial spiritual battles are some of the valleys through which God's hand of mercy has led Kelly and Ed. She has done battle with spiritual wickedness as the enemy has tried to cause division and strife in the ranks of various missions entities. One particularly trying time came about when the leader of an international school proved to be a wolf in sheep's clothing. Kelly worked at the school, and it was extraordinarily hard for her, a natural people-pleaser, to blow the whistle on false teaching. Yet, her commitment to the truth of Scripture compelled her, and the Good Shepherd sustained her. She adds: "God helped us to stand on the truth and he brought us through. When we returned to the United States in 2015, I thought I would never get over the pain that I experienced. Yet, God is so good, and he has completely healed me. When we recently returned to Nepal for the dedication of the New Testament translation project in the language with which we worked, God showed me that our years of labor were not in vain." From the kitchen table of a neighbor's home to the dirty streets of Nepal, God's grace has sustained Kelly for many years. The beauty of the Savior and the grace he offered were, for Kelly, irresistible. It has been her joy and delight to bring the good news of his grace to the far corners of the world.

ADVICE TO YOUNGER READERS: Hide God's Word in your heart, meditate on it, and memorize it. It is a true treasure, so store it up! Love the Lord with all your heart, mind, soul, and strength. Set aside daily time alone with God in which you meditate on his Word, pray, and worship him.

FAVORITE PASSAGE: "Now to him who is able to keep you from stumbling and to present you blameless before the presence of his glory with great joy, to the only God, our Savior, through Jesus Christ our Lord, be glory, majesty, dominion, and authority, before all time and now and forever. Amen" (Jude 24-25).

DAY 21

NANCY (B. 1957)

THE SPIRIT AND THE WORD

In the vast fields and rolling hillsides of northwestern Minnesota, Nancy was blessed to grow up on a farm nestled near a small, quaint town. Her family had deep roots in Norway and Sweden, so it was only natural that they would regularly attend a local Lutheran congregation. Although paedobaptism (i.e., infant baptism) and confirmation classes were a staple in their family's church, Nancy's parents wanted her and their other girls to get more exposure to gospel-centered teaching and preaching. So, her entire family attended a Lutheran summer camp that focused heavily on evangelism and unpacking the gospel for the campers. In addition to her treasured time at summer camp, Nancy also attended youth conferences, evangelistic outreach events, and weekly Bible study for high school students. She loved being involved with religious activities, but her grasp of God's grace in the gospel of Christ remained weak.

Following in her sister's footsteps, Nancy attended a large Bible college in the Twin Cities metro. Nancy recalls: "It was there I learned how to study my Bible. I don't know the exact moment I became a believer, but I remember I accepted as absolute truth what was taught in my Bible classes. I believed that I was a sinner and that Jesus Christ died for my sins, and my faith grew." Millions of believers through the ages have experienced what

Nancy encountered on campus—the power of God's Word. The psalmist declares: "Your testimonies are wonderful; therefore my soul keeps them. The unfolding of your words gives light; it imparts understanding to the simple" (Ps. 119:129-130). The Lord ignited a passion for his Word in Nancy's heart that could not be extinguished. From Bible college, she went on to attend a large state university and quickly became involved with an on-campus Bible study. As she dug deeply into Scripture, she sharpened her own theological convictions. Upon completing her degree, she moved back to the Twin Cities where she attended a large but faithful church. Not only did she find the food her soul desperately needed, but she also found the man who would become her beloved husband and friend. As Nancy takes inventory of her life and the myriad ways that God has preserved her faith, she is overwhelmed. The promises of Romans 8 have become sweeter than honey to Nancy: "For I am sure that neither death nor life, nor angels nor rulers, nor things present nor things to come, nor powers, nor height nor depth, nor anything else in all creation, will be able to separate us from the love of God in Christ Jesus our Lord" (Rom. 8:38-39). She marvels and says: "I am humbled and grateful for how God orchestrated all the people and events in my life to lead to my salvation. I am also humbled by his grace, kindness, faithfulness, and love for me despite all my failings."

God's grace endured, carrying Nancy through the inevitable ups and downs of life. With her husband, Gary, she embarked on the adventure of international adoption. The Lord blessed Nancy and Gary with two little girls from China. She loved visiting the home country of her precious girls and experiencing its unique culture and food. She notes: "Our lives were enriched through adoption, and we were honored that the Lord had chosen us to be the parents of these children." Yet, parenting has also brought numerous trials into Nancy's life. The Word that she fed into her mind and soul through the years has sustained her through many seasons. Nancy's response is one of gladness that bears the aroma of wisdom: "We believe that God is sovereign, and this is what he intended for us—and it is all for his glory. His grace is shown to us in the resources he has given us." The flesh wilts under the pressure of constantly dying to one's own agenda, but the Spirit of God works through the Word of God to help us endure with joy.

ADVICE TO YOUNGER READERS: Your life on earth is painfully short, so read the book of Ecclesiastes. Do not waste your life in pursuing the pleasures of this world. Focus on fearing the Lord, his precepts, and obey him out of a heart of gratitude for what he has done for you in Christ Jesus.

FAVORITE PASSAGE: "Why are you cast down, O my soul, and why are you in turmoil within me? Hope in God; for I shall again praise him, my salvation and my God. My soul is cast down within me; therefore I remember you from the land of Jordan and of Hermon, from Mount Mizar. Deep calls to deep at the roar of your waterfalls; all your breakers and your waves have gone over me. By day the Lord commands his steadfast love, and at night his song is with me, a prayer to the God of my life" (Ps. 42:5-8).

DAY 22

RICH (B. 1949)

GLORIOUS GRACE IN THE GREATEST EPISTLE

Although every book, chapter, verse, and letter in sacred Scripture is equally inspired and authoritative, many theologians through the centuries have noted the peculiar blessings that come with studying the book of Romans. Perhaps it is Paul's *magnum opus*, the letter in which he lays out most clearly and with the most detail his theology and commitment to the gospel of Christ. After all, his voluminous 16-chapter epistle begins with this bold declaration: "For I am not ashamed of the gospel, for it is the power of God for salvation to everyone who believes, to the Jew first and also to the Greek. For in it the righteousness of God is revealed from faith for faith, as it is written, 'The righteous shall live by faith'" (Rom. 1:16-17). Rich grew up in a Christian home and, by God's sovereign grace, came to an understanding of his need for Christ at a young age. With candor, Rich looks back and admits: "I had a child-like faith and understanding of God, the Son, and the Holy Spirit. My faith grew stronger through my 20's, but in my 30's I began seriously studying the book of Romans." During his climb through Paul's mountainous epistle, Rich was gripped by a passion for God's glory: "In the book of Romans, I came to understand the reality of my sin nature, my inherent depravity, and what Jesus did on the cross through the shedding of his blood for my sins."

Rich encountered one of the most explosive passages in all of Scripture. His love of Christ swelled as he came to understand more of what Christ did on the cross. Nowhere does the apostle wax as eloquently as he does in Romans chapter 3: "Whom [Jesus] God put forward as a propitiation by his blood, to be received by faith. This was to show God's righteousness, because in his divine forbearance he had passed over former sins. It was to show his righteousness at the present time, so that he might be just and the justifier of the one who has faith in Jesus" (Rom. 3:25-26). The Lord used the book of Romans in a peculiar way in Rich's life. A brief survey of its contents quickly reveals why it had such a formative impact on Rich's thinking, feeling, and living:

- "Now to the one who works, his wages are not counted as a gift but as his due. And to the one who does not work but believes in him who justifies the ungodly, his faith is counted as righteousness" (Rom. 4:4-5).
- "Therefore, since we have been justified by faith, we have peace with God through our Lord Jesus Christ" (Rom. 5:1).
- "There is therefore now no condemnation for those who are in Christ Jesus" (Rom. 8:1).
- "For I consider that the sufferings of this present time are not worth comparing with the glory that is to be revealed to us" (Rom. 8:18).
- "So faith comes from hearing, and hearing through the word of Christ" (Rom. 10:17).
- "Oh, the depth of the riches and wisdom and knowledge of God! How unsearchable are his judgments and how inscrutable his ways! For who has known the mind of the Lord, or who has been his counselor? Or who has given a gift to him that he might be repaid? For from him and through him and to him are all things. To him be glory forever. Amen" (Rom. 11:33-36).

In addition to the bedrock of grace that Romans brought into Rich's life, the Lord also blessed him with his wife and co-laborer in Christ, Kathy. They served together for nearly a decade mentoring young adults, something that Rich found great delight in doing. Also, the day before he was to marry Kathy, he received an envelope in the mail. After much prayer and hard work, the young husband-to-be was notified that he had been accepted to an Ivy League business school. The Lord blessed Rich's academic pursuits and used the move to the east coast to strengthen his bond to Kathy. God's glorious grace continues to captivate Rich's heart, and the Lord regularly brings him back to the promises of the greatest epistle to strengthen and sustain his soul.

ADVICE TO YOUNGER READERS: Heed God's Word regarding being unequally yoked; this is critical for marriage as well as business. Feed on Scripture, and stay committed to a healthy, Bible-preaching local church with strong, intentional fellowship!

FAVORITE PASSAGE: "What then shall we say to these things? If God is for us, who can be against us? He who did not spare his own Son but gave him up for us all, how will he not also with him graciously give us all things? Who shall bring any charge against God's elect? It is God who justifies" (Rom. 8:31-33).

DAY 23

BETTY (B. 1937)

STEWARDING THE GOSPEL FOR THE NEXT GENERATION

The concept that perplexed Nicodemus has befuddled many people in the centuries since his late-night meeting with the Messiah. John records the exchange: "Jesus answered him, 'Truly, truly, I say to you, unless one is born again he cannot see the kingdom of God.' Nicodemus said to him, 'How can a man be born when he is old? Can he enter a second time into his mother's womb and be born?'" (Jn. 3:3-4). The same look of consternation came across Betty's face. At the age of 14 she attended a youth rally and placed her faith in Christ, though she was never discipled. She went on to marry her beloved Jim, and she gave him a Bible to ensure that he came to treasure the Christ that she knew. Both of them had a rudimentary knowledge of Scripture, but they hungered for deeper knowledge of God. Betty remained plagued by a desire to understand what Scripture says about being born again (i.e., regeneration). The couple began building a life together, attending church, and were blessed with two children. Yet, the gnawing question that plagued the wide-eyed Pharisee continued to swirl in Betty's mind.

God blessed Betty with a few Christian friends who shared her hunger for the meat of Scripture. In those days, reel-to-reel audio machines were the height of technological convenience for those who wanted to listen to lectures and sermons from the comfort of their homes. After consuming hours of expository preaching and deep biblical studies, Betty and Jim began teaching their children what they were learning. From the group's efforts to catechize their families in the riches of God's Word sprang a movement. Soon, their home was filled on Sundays with children and their parents who longed to quench their spiritual thirst. At one point during this time, these families hosted up to 11 Bible study and prayer meetings per week in various locations. The group of hungry seekers continued to grow as did their need of a biblically qualified pastor.

A man answered the group's call for a shepherd and came to serve as the pastor for the burgeoning congregation. What began as a simple Bible study would, through the decades, grow to become Redeemer Bible Church in Minnetonka, MN. Betty delights to walk into the sanctuary and see many believers of various ages hearing God's Word preached and responding with heartfelt worship to the Savior. Though it is primarily a work of God's grace, the fact remains that numerous generations of Christians have been nourished by God's Word because young believers opened their homes and their Bibles with a handful of others. As should be expected, Betty has witnessed her beloved church suffer through various seasons of trial. Yet, she continues to marvel at God's enduring grace as the gospel goes forth in power to the next generation.

As she ages, Betty also has come to relish God's enduring grace in her own life. The words of the apostle Paul get sweeter with every passing day and every new ache and pain: "For I consider that the sufferings of this present time are not worth comparing with the glory that will be revealed to us" (Rom. 8:18). Anyone who spends time with Betty knows that she, like so many stalwart saints, bleeds Scripture. The Word of God has become so intimately woven into the fabric of her mind and heart that her speech and her prayers are filled with large portions of Scripture. She finds daily comfort when she "wakes up knowing that God is sovereign." The Word of God that Betty has sought to know and steward for others is replete with this theme: he works all things to the counsel of his perfect, holy will (Eph. 1:11). The truth of God's supremacy and specific passages of Scripture have provided Betty with the necessary weapons to fight against routine battles with depression. Like the psalmist, Betty has learned the value of preaching to her own heart when darkness falls: "Why are you cast down, O my soul, and why are you in turmoil within me? Hope in God; for I shall again praise him, my salvation and my God" (Ps. 42:5-6). Only eternity will reveal how many people have been pulled like brands from the fire by hearing the gospel, a message maintained through Betty's humble efforts. Many generations have been blessed by God's grace flowing through Betty's life, and she intends to finish her race by stewarding the gospel for the next generation.

ADVICE TO YOUNGER READERS: Take it from someone who has, by God's grace, put it into practice—read your Bible *every* day. Ask God to search your heart and keep a short account of your sin with him. Also, preach the gospel to yourself daily so that you fall in love with Jesus over and over again.

FAVORITE PASSAGE: "For God, who said, 'Let light shine out of darkness,' has shone in our hearts to give the light of the knowledge of the glory of God in the face of Jesus Christ" (2 Cor. 4:6).

DAY 24

AUDREY (B. 1934)

BE STILL, MY ANXIOUS HEART

Among the many issues addressed in the Protestant Reformation was the critical matter of *assurance*. Can we know for certain that we are saved? Can we rest our heads at night with the confidence that our souls are secure despite our routine failures? Although the magisterial reformers provided overwhelming biblical evidence that genuine believers can experience assurance, many still struggle with ongoing doubts. Audrey was one of the many Christians who routinely battled against insecurity. One question constantly rattled in her mind: *How can I know for certain that I am going to heaven?* In her desperation, Audrey went to a pastor to seek counsel. Their exchange remains one her saddest memories. Rather than pointing the young lady to the finished work of Christ on her behalf, the minister said: "Well, Audrey, I don't know if I can answer that question, even for myself." Dejected and anxious, she walked out of his office with her doubts, rather than her joy, intact.

Audrey continued to plead with the Lord, as best she understood him, to help her understand what salvation means. When her young daughter asked for a playdate with a friend, Audrey agreed without knowing that God would use that seemingly banal event to change her life. When the girl's mother arrived to pick her up, Audrey invited her in for tea. The woman declined, telling Audrey that she needed to attend a Bible study at her church. Audrey's heart dropped as she hoped that she had finally met someone who could answer her question. So, with the passion only years of longing can foment, she launched her inquiry. Audrey leaned toward the girl's mother, saying: "People tell me I will go to heaven because I am a good person, but I do not believe I can be good enough. What do you think?" The young mother joyfully shared the gospel with Audrey, telling her the bad news that prepared her heart to hear the good news: "For all have sinned and fall short of the glory of God, and are justified by his grace as a gift, through the redemption that is in Christ Jesus" (Rom. 3:23-24). As the woman explained to Audrey that no one is good enough to merit salvation from an eternally holy God, Audrey's heart sprang open to receive Christ as Savior and Lord. Audrey attended a number of Bible studies at the lady's house where she continued to hear the gospel and grew in her understanding that salvation is by grace alone, through faith alone, in Christ alone. Her anxious soul finally found rest in the arms of her Savior, the Lord Jesus Christ.

With her new, unshakable joy and confidence, the hues of Audrey's life took on new and vibrant color. Her marriage to Lowell was sweeter, and the two began making plans to build their dream home. A lover of Christ himself, Lowell delighted to work alongside his bride in the construction of the house, most of which he did himself. Audrey recalls: "We have countless stories of how we were able to be gracious to one another in the building of our home. We had strong opinions about silly things like carpet and paint, but those memories are sweet as we look back and realize that God was teaching us not to make mountains out of mole hills." After decades of joyful, God-centered marriage and parenthood, Lowell became ill. She cared for his needs as best she could, but his medical demands proved to be too much for in-home care. The Lord used precious friends, Wanda and Judy, to help Audrey find a nursing home to which she felt comfortable sending her beloved Lowell. As Lowell's condition worsened, Audrey prepared herself to say goodbye. The words of the psalmist reminded her of God's tender care of his ailing children: "Precious in the sight of the Lord is the death of his saints" (Ps. 116:15). Lowell went to be with Christ in 2021, and his service was attended by many friends and family. As scenes from their life together played on the screens in the church, Audrey experienced the paradox that the apostle spoke of: "as sorrowful, yet always rejoicing" (2 Cor. 6:10). If God had not used an impromptu evangelist to share the gospel with her one afternoon many years prior, Audrey would not have the assurance to help her beloved face death or contemplate her own departure. But she can now say, *be still, my anxious heart.*

ADVICE TO YOUNGER READERS: On your life's journey, there will undoubtedly be many obstacles. Many of the paths the Lord leads us down are scary and hard; we often feel out of control. But don't be frightened. God makes himself intimately known on those paths, and the blessings you will experience are immeasurable!

FAVORITE PASSAGE: "The Lord is my shepherd; I shall not want. He makes me lie down in green pastures. He leads me beside still waters. He restores my soul. He leads me in paths of righteousness for his name's sake. Even though I walk through the valley of the shadow of death, I will fear no evil, for you are with me; your rod and your staff, they comfort me" (Ps. 23:1-4).

DAY 25

MIKE (B. 1950)

THE JOY OF JUSTIFICATION

There is a world of difference between gaining righteousness and being given righteousness. The difference is as vast as the chasm from one end of eternity to the other. It is no wonder that the doctrine of justification (i.e., being declared righteous by God) is central to the Bible's story of redemption. In the minds of many Jews, Abraham was saved because he, being a moral and law-keeping man, earned a righteous standing before God. However, the apostle Paul, himself a Jew, knew better: "What then shall we say was gained by Abraham, our forefather according to the flesh? For if Abraham was justified by works, he has something to boast about, but not before God. For what the does the Scripture say? 'Abraham believed God, and it was counted to him as righteousness'" (Rom. 4:1-3). Though he attended church as a young man, Mike never heard this gospel. He recalls: "I grew up in a mainline Protestant church where the doctrinal teaching was weak, so as a teenager I had a deficient understanding of the gospel, salvation, and the deity of Christ." Where there is no understanding of justification by grace, there is no lasting joy.

In the fall of 1976, Mike graduated from college and began attending a new church where he took the time to read the entire Bible. In that season of life, the Lord opened Mike's eyes to the realities of his own depravity and the glorious work of Jesus Christ on his behalf. The gospel cascaded from Mike's mind and filled his heart; he was truly born again. The difference in his life was noticeable: "My family could see a change in me, and for the first time in my life I had joy—God's joy through his Spirit. I once was lost, but then I was found. I had been alienated from God because of my sin, but now I am reconciled to God and saved from his wrath through Christ. He delivered me from the domain of darkness and transferred me to the kingdom of his beloved Son!" In short, Mike realized the full implications of being declared righteous by faith in Christ. His was a joy born out of justification.

One of the ways God helped Mike understand the riches of the gospel came in 1995. A Canadian pastor visited his church and heralded the gospel from the books of Romans and Galatians. A flood of joy overwhelmed Mike as the young preacher unpacked the doctrine of justification. In his own words, Mike gushes with gladness: "I understood that not only did Christ's death pay for my sins, but that his perfect obedience was credited to me at salvation. Instead of striving to earn God's acceptance by keeping the law, I was accepted totally because of Christ's perfect righteousness imputed to me by faith in him. That was a very powerful and burden-lifting moment in my life, and it launched me into a robust study of God's Word that continues to this day."

Knowing that his standing before God is secure enabled Mike to face numerous health challenges in his life. One of the hardest seasons of his life came in 2006 when he contracted a very serious infection that required hospitalization. Spending a few days in the Intensive Care Unit, Mike was very close to death. Yet, he found joy and peace because he knew that he remained justified and safe in union with Christ. Mike knew that, by faith in Jesus, Paul's promise was his own: "For I am sure that neither death nor life, nor angels nor rulers, nor things present nor things to come, nor powers, nor height nor depth, nor anything else in all creation, will be able to separate us from the love of God in Christ Jesus our Lord" (Rom. 8:38-39). Although the doctrines of the Reformation can be voluminous and deep, they often lead to heartfelt, humble worship and adoration of God. Mike is no exception. In the place of anxious striving came joyful obedience. In the place of white-knuckle wishing came warmhearted singing. The joy of having a real, abiding, and intimate relationship with the Lord Jesus Christ produced the sweet fruit of joy in Mike's life, an aroma that caught the attention of everyone around him. Happiness is often transient, but joy is a different breed. As Mike has drilled further into the mine of God's Word, he has uncovered increasing amounts of gospel gold. In doing so, he continues to experience the joy of justification.

ADVICE TO YOUNGER READERS: Hold fast to the truth of God's Word. Even though the gospel is being attacked on every side by the culture, it remains the power of God for salvation for all who believe. I hope the next generation of believers love and treasure Christ more than anything. If that is to happen, they must prioritize time in his Word.

FAVORITE PASSAGE: "And we all, with unveiled face, beholding the glory of the Lord, are being transformed into the same image from one degree of glory to another. For this comes from the Lord who is the Spirit" (2 Cor. 3:18).

DAY 26

PAT (B. 1953)

LESS IS MORE

Whenever someone describes an experience as *interesting*, one can usually assume that there is more to the story. If a wife asks her husband what he thought of dinner and he replies, "It was…interesting," there will undoubtedly be fireworks. This is precisely how Pat describes her upbringing, and for good reason. Her mother was a devout Roman Catholic while her father was committed to Christian Science for most of his life before coming to genuine faith in Jesus Christ. Pat even recalls: "I was the one in our family who was supposed to grow up and become a nun." Although she was somewhat intrigued by the idea of spending her days studying and serving God, she was never settled with the tenets of Roman Catholicism or Christian Science. Looking back, Pat states: "When I was seven years old and about to make my first confession (which was required to take one's first communion), I pondered why I needed to tell someone other than God about my sins. I remember clearly walking around outside of St. Gertrude Church in Illinois and hearing the Lord tell me that there was more." More of what? Pat had to know.

She never became a nun. In fact, she lived a kind of wilderness experience in which she stifled the beckoning of conscience and lived in open rebellion to God's Word. In all her disobedience, God's grace endured. She notes: "Though I never received the wrath my sinful behavior deserved, I persisted in my obstinance. But God also persisted in seeking me out." She seemed to always know that there was more, but she did not realize that it would require less. Pat slowly came to realize that salvation requires less of our efforts and more of Christ's perfect obedience in our place; it requires less of ourselves and more of the person and work of Jesus. To be precise, Pat began to understand that her salvation was wholly dependent on God's grace. Despite growing up around religious trappings, it was not until her adult years that Pat came to know and relish the truth that captured Martin Luther centuries before: "For in [the gospel] the righteousness of God is revealed from faith for faith, as it is written, 'The righteous shall live by faith'" (Rom. 1:17). Through her involvement with a local Bible study and the counsel of godly friends, Pat fully repented of her sin and placed her trust in Jesus Christ alone. Less of her gave way to more of Christ.

The God who saved her also promised to keep her to the end (Jude 24-25). This blood-bought promise would prove to be a firm foundation upon which Pat could stand. In the frame of one year, Pat's father died, her mother developed Alzheimer's disease and began to forget who Pat was, and her beloved husband also died suddenly from an aneurysm. Through all these various trials, Pat wept in grief while also finding fresh joy in an ever-present Savior. Trials have taught her to pray for God's will to be done rather than her will. She found that the deeper she dug into the gospel, the more her desires were consumed by one passion—for God to be glorified. Moreover, twenty years of regular involvement with a local Bible study has been used of God to strengthen Pat's faith and rivet her eyes on the person and work of Christ. The genuineness of her faith has been made clear through painful circumstances. This is precisely what Paul outlined: "Through [Christ] we have also obtained access by faith into this grace in which we stand, and we rejoice in hope of the glory of God. Not only that, but we rejoice in our sufferings, knowing that suffering produces endurance, and endurance produces character, and character produces hope, and hope does not put us to shame, because God's love has been poured into our hearts through the Holy Spirit who has been given to us" (Rom. 5:2-5).

As he promised in Ephesians 2:10, God has shown Pat that her trials were to give way to good works that he had prepared for her to do. Speaking of the year in which the trials came, Pat recalls: "God used those trials to strengthen me and to help me grow in my faith. Due to my mother's illness, I learned to serve the Lord by facilitating worship services for senior citizens in care homes. Through the loss of my husband, I learned to be a grief group leader. God does indeed use our suffering and pain to strengthen and refine us." Less really is more. Less focus on what we offer God and a greater focus on what he has offered up for us in his Son is the key to a vibrant, personal relationship with him.

ADVICE TO YOUNGER READERS: Stay in his Word and listen for his voice to be found there. Pray about *everything*, and make sure you are part of a healthy, gospel-saturated church.

FAVORITE PASSAGE: "Trust in the Lord with all your heart, and do not lean on your own understanding. In all your ways acknowledge him, and he will make straight your paths" (Prov. 3:5-6).

DAY 27

BRITTON (B. 1959)

SINGING THROUGH SUFFERING

Two men, Paul and Silas, found themselves in the bowels of a Philippian prison with their feet securely fastened in stocks. While many would be fraught with hopelessness, the men battled their suffering by singing. Luke records the incident: "About midnight Paul and Silas were praying and singing hymns to God, and the prisoners were listening to them" (Acts 16:25). Although it has never been accompanied by earthquakes or angelic visitations, Britton has found singing the truth of God's Word amid trials is a powerful means of grace in his life. Yet, the impetus to sing praises to God found its genesis many years before those trials came into Britton's life. The sound of God's truth being vocalized in song and harmony impacted him in kid's choir. He looks back and recounts:

> I remember distinctly at the age of four being told to go to my room for quiet time. Instead, I went outside and played with my neighbor. When my mom confronted me, I boldly lied to her. She warned me that my sins would find me out. At the age of five, I truly learned and understood that my sins offended a holy God. I also came to understand that Jesus died in my place because he loved me. Those two truths laid a solid foundation for me as I increased in my knowledge and understanding of spiritual truths. So, when I was convicted

> of my sin as a teen, it was both humbling and hope-giving to go to God in song and seek his forgiveness.

As a teenager, Britton had difficulty making and keeping friends. Yet, the Lord worked through this period of his life to draw him into close fellowship with his siblings as well as his church family. Along with his family, Britton engaged in private worship in their home in addition to corporate worship with the gathered congregation. He recalls with delight: "A favorite memory of mine is on Sunday evenings when we were able to choose a favorite hymn to sing. I loved the fact that truth was put to music." Britton's experience is a common theme in Scripture. In addition to Paul and Silas in prison, Paul goes on to note the connection between truth and singing: "Let the word of Christ dwell in you richly, teaching and admonishing one another in all wisdom, singing psalms and hymns and spiritual songs, with thankfulness in your hearts to God" (Col. 3:16). Tuning his heart to the key of the gospel would prove to be a necessary step in bringing Britton through the valleys that lie ahead of him.

In addition to the pain of isolation in high school, periods of unemployment have proven to be some of the most trying times in his life. With their eighth child on the way, he recalls: "God's providence had Jan and I memorize Matthew chapter 6 together. God sustained us through that period of joblessness and, not long after, blessed me with a new job. When other seasons of unemployment came, we could truly see God's provision and grace as we trusted his promises. It was an opportunity for our children to witness it and praise God. The Lord eventually provided a good job that used my field of study." Another blessing that God gave to Britton is his wife, Jan. The two of them have taught parenting classes together and have helped other Christian couples make critical decisions about their children's education options. Helping other believers learn to walk in daily submission to Christ remains one of Britton's greatest delights. It is not uncommon to see him praying for younger believers in church on Sunday morning.

Just as the sound of singing echoed from the inner prison of Philippi many centuries ago, the tunes of Christ-exalting hymns and songs can be heard echoing from the heart and mouth of Britton. God's enduring grace is often carried into our lives on the wings of a melody. Britton highlights this fact: "I remember in the midst of suffering hearing the lyrics of a particular song which lifted me up and changed both my perspective and the course of my actions." Although his life has been marked by seasons of uncertainty, the immovable truth of the gospel has delighted Britton's heart and overflowed in songs of praise. He aims to fan the flames of joy in others, pointing them to the Savior who is worthy of our worship!

ADVICE TO YOUNGER READERS: Remember that life is hard, but also remember that God is good. So be faithful in the little things. If the Lord gives you children, spend individual time with each child, delighting in them and showing them that you enjoy them. There are many things you can do with your children, but one thing that uniquely encourages them is for you to bless them before bedtime.

FAVORITE PASSAGE: "Bless the Lord, O my soul, and all that is within me, bless his holy name! Bless the Lord, O my soul, and forget not all his benefits" (Ps. 103:1-2).

DAY 28

DENNIS (B. 1948)

LEARNING TO SHARE THE SPOTLIGHT

An unassuming townhome sits nestled in the far corner of a wooded lot. Thousands of cars drive by each day, stirring up the freshly fallen snow as they disappear into the distance. A gray-haired man sits at the end of a massive, solid oak table. With his Bible and notebook open before him, he sits in the silence of his home and engages in his daily routine of scribbling thoughts and prayers into his journal, occasionally bowing his head to commune with the Lord who has sustained him through a fascinating yet tumultuous life. Few people would guess that the contemplative older man at the table was once a renowned stage actor, producer, and entertainment mogul. A glance at his personal resume reveals his work ethic: president and CEO of a private entertainment company, producer to major productions with national exposure, actor at Minneapolis' coveted Guthrie theatre, and more. The list of stars he has worked with over the decades include Henry Fonda, Robin Williams, Neil Sedaka, Leonard Nimoy, and Cloris Leachman. In addition, he has produced another major stage production on the life of Charles Dickens, a feat that gave him the opportunity to meet the Queen at Buckingham Palace along with the Duke of Edinburgh. As if meeting Her Majesty was not enough of an accomplishment, he also completed 28 marathons that spanned six continents. Yet, there are some glaring omissions from his illustrious career that include drug use (cocaine), sexual promiscuity, three marriages, and a 21-day drug rehab stay. Dennis, the man sitting silently at his table, is a fascinating specimen indeed.

In 1964, Dennis attended a large Billy Graham crusade. Although he heard and understood the gospel, the allurement of notoriety and money pulled him away. As he built his career as a stage actor and media producer, the money and fame indeed came to Dennis. Unfortunately, a million heartaches also came with them. Rather than delighting himself in eternal pleasures, Dennis chose the fleeting delight of sin (Ps. 16:11; Heb. 11:24-25). But the Good Shepherd, who vowed to leave the 99 in search of the one wayward sheep, pursued Dennis through all his rebellion and sin. It was a severe kind of grace that brought him to the rehab center in 1987. Recalling that time in his life, Dennis confesses: "I always believed in a god of some kind. Even as a youngster I would lie in bed and wonder what would happen to me after death. It was a very disquieting feeling. In the rehab center, I had no job, no wife, and no home. I had no healthy relationships, and I had no way of identifying myself without the things that were now stripped from me." More than anything, Dennis had a worship problem. He had to learn to share the spotlight. He had to learn that his was a supporting role, and God was the main player.

In rehab, there were no more distractions. There were no scripts, no stages, no press conferences, and no after parties. Dennis had exactly what he needed: time, silence, and a Bible. As his shaky hand turned the pages of Scripture, he landed in the book of Galatians. The passage that God used to awaken Dennis to his need of a Savior was found in chapter 5: "But I say, walk by the Spirit, and you will not gratify the desires of the flesh. For the desires of the flesh are against the Spirit, and the desires of the Spirit are against the flesh, for these are opposed to each other, to keep you from doing the things you want to do" (Gal. 5:16-17). God's grace endured, bringing Dennis to a place where he joyfully confessed: "I have been crucified with Christ. It is no longer I who live, but Christ who lives in me. And the life I now live in the flesh I live by faith in the Son of God, who loved me and gave himself for me" (Gal. 2:20). After completing rehab, Dennis joined a church and was promptly baptized. God's grace has preserved his faith through the decades, and Dennis now uses his many connections in the entertainment industry to share the good news of the gospel with people who rarely interact with devoted Christians. Even when he lost funding for a major stage production and was diagnosed with Parkinson's disease, he continued to lead a men's Bible study. Trials have taught Dennis to share the spotlight with the only One worthy to receive it, something he now gladly does.

ADVICE TO YOUNGER READERS: Be careful to make sure you surround yourself with wise mentors. Be on guard against the attacks of the enemy. Be ever mindful of the temporal nature of things in this life. Also, find another mature believer with whom you can be honest and transparent.

FAVORITE PASSAGE: "But he said to me, 'My grace is sufficient for you, for my power is made perfect in weakness.' Therefore I will boast all the more gladly of my weaknesses, so that the power of Christ may rest upon me. For the sake of Christ, then, I am content with weaknesses, insults, hardships, persecutions, and calamities. For when I am weak, then I am strong" (2 Cor. 12:9-10).

DAY 29

JAN (B. 1957)

LOSING AND GAINING A FATHER

Millions of professing Christians recite what is known as The Lord's Prayer. The opening line is familiar, but its depth of meaning is often lost: "Our *Father* in heaven" (Matt. 6:9, emphasis added). In light of the Bible's witness regarding the sinful, depraved, rebellious, and estranged status of mankind (Rom. 1:18, 6:23), to be able to address God Almighty as Father is no small thing. Yet, this is at the heart of the wonder of the gospel of Christ: "For all who are led by the Spirit of God are sons of God. For you did not receive the spirit of slavery to fall back into fear, but you have received the Spirit of adoption as sons, by whom we cry, 'Abba! Father!' The Spirit himself bears witness with our spirit that we are children of God" (Rom. 8:14-16). This concept would, in time, become a precious promise for young Jan. At the tender age of nine, her father died. Thereafter, her mother allowed Jan to decide if she wanted to attend church. For a season, she attended a United Church of Christ, but the progressively liberal congregation offered no biblical comfort and Jan soon stopped going. In losing her father, Jan began to lose hope too.

In her teens, Jan was enrolled in a private school and soon began attending an in-school Christian fellowship. During the ministry's Halloween event, Jan found a much-needed group of friends with whom she began attending a different church from the one in which she had been raised. Her friends proved to be a means of grace in Jan's life as they stuck together through high school, holding one another accountable and offering mutual encouragement. Though she certainly heard the gospel in that season of life, it was not until she attended college that Jan began studying God's Word seriously. She attended an on-campus InterVarsity meeting, and the Lord opened her eyes to the beauty of Christ. Jan was marvelously born again. The fatherless girl who walked away from church was captivated by the one who gave her open access to a loving heavenly Father. She recalls: "My walk toward God was a slow progression, and I know it was a miracle that he opened my eyes to see my sinfulness and my need for a Savior."

In her marriage, Jan has been blessed with eight children. Motherhood has been the crowning joy of Jan's life, but it has also been the fountainhead of many trials. There is an unsurprisingly heavy financial burden that accompanies large families. In hindsight, Jan sees that her venture into motherhood was bookended by seasons of unemployment for her husband. Jan was in graduate school when her husband lost his job with a reputable company. The same day that her husband came home and told her that he had been laid off, Jan told him that she was pregnant with their first child. Seventeen years later, the tragic scene repeated itself. With seven children ranging in ages 3-17, Jan's husband was again laid off on the same day she announced that she was pregnant with their eighth child. Sometimes, as William Cowper noted, God's providence comes in gray clouds that obscure the face of our heavenly Father, at least for a while.

As Jan learned to lean upon the Lord for daily grace and strength, he slowly cultivated a heart of wisdom within her. Pointing her children as well as herself to Christ amid trial opened the door for Jan to encourage other families who faced similar struggles. Alongside her husband, she was blessed with the opportunity to teach parenting classes over an 18-year period. Not only was Jan able to exhort other parents, but she also found wonderful accountability for her own parenting. It is a testimony to God's kindness that the girl who lost her father grew to be a mentor for parents. God's grace has endured in Jan's life, a grace that she has labored to make known to her children and to other believers with families. Though she lost her earthly father, Jan has come to relish the words found in John's first epistle: "See what kind of love the Father has given to us, that we should be called children of God; and so we are. The reason why the world does not know us is that it did not know him. Beloved, we are God's children now" (1 Jn. 3:1-2). Jan lost a father, but she also gained a Father. By faith in Christ, she has been permanently adopted into God's family.

ADVICE TO YOUNGER READERS: If you are blessed with children, raise kids that you enjoy. Be sure to set reasonable guidelines for them. Delight in the Lord yourself so that they see that Christ is your treasure.

FAVORITE PASSAGE: "The steadfast love of the Lord never ceases; his mercies never come to an end; they are new every morning; great is your faithfulness. 'The Lord is my portion,' says my soul, 'therefore I will hope in him'" (Lam. 3:22-24).

DAY 30

CARL (B. 1961)

HELPED BY HEROES

Comic books and action movies have become monolithic money makers through the efforts of Hollywood and its marketing machinery. From Superman to Batman, there is an ever-increasing roster of superheroes from which to choose. Although they lack special powers and are as sinful and in need of grace as anyone else, Christians often have heroes too. These are usually gifted, faithful preachers and teachers whom God uses to help his people grow in their knowledge of his Word. The entirety of Hebrews chapter 11 is built around the idea of looking to the imperfect lives of other people who trusted God's Word and, by his grace, made it home to glory. So, Christians do *not* worship their heroes, but they are certainly thankful for them. In Carl's life, God used some unknown heroes as well as some well-known heroes to help him grow in his understanding of the gospel.

When he was young, Carl attended a Billy Graham crusade in Dallas. Though there would be many fits and starts in his walk with the Lord, Carl credits this event as being the place where he first began to understand and embrace the basic tenets of the gospel. Through his teens, Carl was sporadically involved with local youth groups, but he found himself coasting. After a while, his pursuit of God cooled, and his vocational pursuits eclipsed his passion for the Lord. The snare of comfort and worldly pursuits took hold of Carl, and he needed to be rescued. The Lord would send another hero into his life, but not until a long journey through a spiritual desert.

Carl met and married Dee Dee, and his career took them to Singapore. While there, Carl made new friends and walked alongside many of them as they endured their own trials. After the death of one of his young friends, Carl began attending a local church. Yet, Singapore was not the only residence that God intended for Carl. His career brought him back to the United States, but he was still far away from Texas. In Minnesota, he found a vibrant church and developed Christ-centered friendships. His season of spiritual dryness began to give way to some precipitation as Carl threw himself into Bible study and meaningful fellowship. In a small group meeting, Carl realized that the Good Shepherd was pursuing him and would not let him go. As Carl leaned into his Bible studies, he found that he was being helped all along: "Not that I have already obtained this or am already perfect, but I press on to make it my own, because Christ Jesus has made me his own" (Phil. 3:12). It was during this period of Carl's life that God sent another hero, one that Carl would never meet in person yet would prove critical to his understanding of God's character. Through the ministry of R. C. Sproul, Carl grew exponentially in his understating of and love for God's absolute sovereignty over all things. Sproul's passion was to awaken the church to the holiness and grandeur of God, and it seems that his goal obtained in Carl's life. With a newfound passion to study God's Word and hear it proclaimed expositionally, Carl and Dee Dee came to Redeemer Bible Church.

Bowing to God's sovereignty and trusting in his providence to work all things for good for those who love him (Rom. 8:28-29), Carl found peace to endure a painful season. While working in California to build his career, Carl traveled home to Minnesota every other week to be with his family. Not surprisingly, this arrangement put tremendous stress upon his wife and children. The strain of his absence brought his family to a crisis point, so Carl humbled himself and quit his job. Though choosing his family's wellbeing over his career has been difficult at times, Carl has no regrets and continues to trust in his heavenly Father's grace to sustain and provide for him. He states, "God humbled me, and it hurt. He continues to humble me. It is for my good, and I love him for it." From Graham to Sproul to his kindhearted sister, God has placed many heroes in Carl's life, fallible though they may be. Yet, there is one primary hero in Carl's story—the Lord Jesus Christ. God uses many means to bless his people, but the fountainhead of all blessings is the person and work of his Son. God's enduring grace has flowed through Carl's life because Carl, by faith alone, is united to God's beloved and enthroned Son.

ADVICE TO YOUNGER READERS: There is often a strong temptation to become complacent and comfortable in your walk with Christ, but you *must* fight it! Do not allow yourself to get lulled into spiritual apathy and laziness. Grounded on God's promise of grace and assistance, strive for growth. The days ahead will undoubtedly test us all, so be ready to stand strong!

FAVORITE PASSAGE: "Therefore, since we are surrounded by so great a cloud of witnesses, let us also lay aside every weight, and sin which clings so closely, and let us run with endurance the race that is set before us, looking to Jesus, the founder and perfecter of our faith, who for the joy that was set before him endured the cross, despising the shame, and is seated at the right hand of the throne of God" (Heb. 12:1-2).

DAY 31

PAULA (B. 1954)

TRADING FILTHY RAGS FOR A RIGHTEOUS ROBE

Humans are insufferably religious. Made in the image of God, we are hardwired to worship. Yet, courtesy of our sinful hearts, we distort this impulse and worship ourselves, created things, and myriad other lesser gods rather than the Creator (Rom. 1:18-32). Without special revelation, humans create gods that they can worship on their own terms. The psalmist explains it this way: "These things you have done, and I have been silent; *you thought that I was one like yourself*" (Ps. 50:21, emphasis added). Young Paula was no exception to this rule. Growing up in an unchurched, non-Christian home, Paula was left to her own devices to decipher what she knew instinctively—God exists. She looked at the pictures in a family Bible and saw religiously themed movies on television. From these scant glances, she cobbled together an understanding of God the best she could. Yet, confusion reigned in her life. She describes it this way: "In this void, I made up my own religion. I felt close to God the Father and I prayed to him, and I even toyed with the idea of embracing Judaism since I did not like the idea of going through a mediator (Jesus) to get to God. I was not very serious about anything religious; getting good grades at school and acting good were my main concerns." Relying on herself, Paula carved out a god that she was comfortable with and that she could assuage with her own efforts. Like every other human being throughout history, Paula settled for idolatry.

The Lord intervened in a powerful way to call his beloved Paula away from the dangers of false religion. In her senior year at college, a Christian friend confronted Paula. The girl lovingly yet boldly told Paula the truth of Isaiah 64:6—all our human efforts to gain righteousness are like filthy rags. Paula winced at the girl's words, declining to embrace her brand of Christianity. But the Lord continued to pursue her through a coworker. Having recently been saved, the friend was bold in his witness for Christ. Since Paula was working the night shift, her friend's influence weighed heavily upon her as she had ample time to contemplate spiritual matters. She recalls: "One night I felt that God showed me the truth of 2 Thessalonians 1:8-9, that hell is eternal separation from his blessed presence. I did not want that! I was never afraid of hell before, but that night I submitted my will to God." With a fresh fear of God kindled in her heart, Paula began looking for a church while in Minnesota for graduate school. In addition to a local congregation, the Lord used a roommate at the university to lead Paula through Bible studies and ground her in the faith. As spring drew near, Paula recounts that "I knew I was a full-fledged Christian by Good Friday when I experienced great joy in knowing that Christ had died for *me* and that the veil in the temple was split when his death gave me true and unfettered access to my heavenly Father."

God's grace sustained Paula through many trials. One such time happened while she was working for an in-home medical care company. She was assigned one of the toughest (and meanest) clients on the roster. The elderly woman would routinely become verbally abusive with Paula, yelling and threatening all those who tried to help her. At times, Paula feared that the woman would physically hurt her or the other workers. As tempting as it was to exchange the cantankerous woman for another client, God's grace urged Paula to come alongside her and love her with the supernatural love of Christ. Trusting in Christ's promise to never leave or forsake his children, Paula took up her cross and spent her days trying to serve and love someone who was unlovely. It took time, but Paula's efforts to make the woman smile paid off. Paula recounts: "She and I would look at National Geographic magazines, watch the Nativity Story together, etc. It became a challenge for me to make her smile. Each time I visited her, I looked forward to bringing her some measure of joy."

Rather than serving others in the hope of earning eternal life, Paula had been freed by the gospel of Jesus Christ to love and serve others without an eye to earthly repayment. She knew that her good works, apart from Christ, were filthy rags. Yet, by faith in Christ and out of love for him, her good works were transformed into acts of thankful worship (Eph. 2:10). It is amazing how much work we can accomplish when we trade the dirty apron of selfish effort for the righteous robes of Christ's perfect obedience.

ADVICE TO YOUNGER READERS: Cling tightly to the Lord and share everything with him. Talk to your heavenly Father and relish his presence.

FAVORITE PASSAGE: "And I am sure of this, that he who began a good work in you will bri ng it to completion at the day of Jesus Christ" (Phil. 1:6).

"Now to him who is able to keep you from stumbling and to present you blameless before the presence of his glory with great joy, to the only God, our Savior, through Jesus Christ our Lord, be glory, majesty, dominion, and authority, before all time and now and forever. Amen" (Jude 24-25).